# INCOMPARABLE

# INCOMPARABLE

Brie & Nikki Bella

GALLERY BOOKS

NEW YORK  LONDON  TORONTO  SYDNEY  NEW DELHI

Gallery Books
An Imprint of Simon & Schuster, Inc.
1230 Avenue of the Americas
New York, NY 10020

Some names and identifying details have been changed,
whether or not so noted in the text.

First Gallery Books hardcover edition May 2020

GALLERY BOOKS and colophon are registered
trademarks of Simon & Schuster, Inc.

For information about special discounts for bulk purchases,
please contact Simon & Schuster Special Sales at 1-866-506-1949
or business@simonandschuster.com.

The Simon & Schuster Speakers Bureau can bring authors to your live event.
For more information or to book an event, contact the Simon & Schuster Speakers
Bureau at 1-866-248-3049 or visit our website at www.simonspeakers.com.

*Interior design by Michelle Marchese*

Manufactured in the United States of America

10   9   8   7   6   5   4   3   2   1

Library of Congress Cataloging-in-Publication Data has been applied for.

ISBN 978-1-5011-9191-6
ISBN 978-1-5011-9193-0 (ebook)

This book is dedicated to our family,
thank you for letting us share our story,
and to our Bella Army, we wouldn't be where
we are at today without you all.

# CONTENTS

# CUTTING THE PROMO

*2019*

San Diego, California

*Brie*

In wrestling, "cutting a promo" is when you get on the mic and create your backstage storyline—whether victim or heel, good guy or bad, beloved or betrayed. Promos are the basis of every great in-ring rivalry, of every highly tuned moment of drama on the mat. It's your chance to make the audience care so that when you step out onto the ramp, you're met with boos or cheers (both equally good, as far as ratings go). Promos are, for the most part, pure fabrication—a device of writers and producers who know how to craft compelling characters, who know how to make good TV.

Because we are twins, they didn't have to use a lot of imagination when they launched us on the main roster. We are identical, so their strategy was to treat us like the same person. They made it about our twindom, not us individually—they made us dress identically, wear our hair identically, move in the ring identically, achieve an identical body composition. This is common in twin culture. In the baby and toddler years, you see it as identical dressing—almost an inability to treat twins differently, to introduce any individuality at all. It's a version of treating everyone the same until they have a chance to express who they are on their own.

When you get older, the cracks in the twindom begin to show. You enter the age of comparison, which lasts your whole life: Which one of you is skinnier, which is smarter, which is better at soccer? Knowing the comparison is coming—that your benchmark is the woman who shared a womb with you, who is sitting next to you—means that you learn how to compete often and easily. We accepted that it was a hallmark of life. The problem is that the very act of comparison typically requires that someone be "better." Someone needs to win.

## Nicole

In many ways, being a twin is like competing against yourself. It's this weird ground where you want to distinguish yourself, you want to win, but it is entwined with love. You don't want the fact that you have won to mean that the person you love the most has lost. I beat my sister at soccer, but only because she was so much better at ballet. She was a better artist, I was better at drama. When you're an identical twin, you start to see your *potential* as a million possibilities—you see in your twin a different outcome from the same egg, not for better or worse. It was easy to then project how we were onto the other girls, to understand that we all have gifts, that some of our qualities can be over-expressed, or not expressed at all. That the worst thing we can do is shut each other down.

It became apparent to both of us that it was all about trade-offs. It was about not having or being everything at the same time, and that the gifts of others are not threats. We came to the understanding that there will always be plenty of beer at the party for everyone. We live in a world of abundance—we just have to choose to see it that way. Your nice house doesn't mean I can't have a nice house, too. The fact that someone else gets something that you want doesn't mean that you won't get it a different time, or that something equally wonderful won't come along that you might want more. As women, we too often feel threatened by other women. We should celebrate what they achieve as a testament of what we can achieve, too.

Comparison of and between women is rampant in our culture, and with that comes this idea and fear of scarcity—that there isn't enough opportunity to go around.

And historically there certainly hasn't been. We witness it firsthand in WWE, where the men far outnumber the women on the roster. But we also see that this reality is shifting. As we along with the other Divas-turned-Superstars have brought more awareness to women's wrestling—through our TV shows, through cutting great promos, and through pure athletic acrobatics and sport—we have brought more young girls and women into the audience. They want to see more of us, and the makeup of the roster is beginning to shift in response. Wrestling is different from other sports in that it is a competition, yes, but it is also a collaboration. We rely on each other to pull off our matches. We rely on each other to make the spectacle look good, to put on a great show. In many ways, we are the perfect illustration of how women helping women only creates more opportunities for all of us—not the other way around. We watched as multiple women experienced success at the very same time. This is not a strange concept to men, but it is certainly not standard thinking for women across the board. We often work at places where there might only be one female executive at a company. We hope that we are part of a cultural movement that helps to change that—where young girls grow up believing that they can do anything, without also having to believe that they're going to have to break down walls to do it.

## Brie

Being part of this movement is a great privilege—and a great responsibility. And that's one of the reasons that Nicole and I felt like it was so important to tell our whole story, from the beginning. It has had incredible bright spots—we both have comfortable lives and incredible careers in WWE that are hopefully not close to being over yet. I have an amazing husband, Bryan, and my daughter, Birdie. If I'm lucky, I'll have another kid; I have every confidence that Nicole is going to be a mother down the road, too. But it has not been easy to get here. Ours is certainly not the worst story you'll ever read in terms of adversity—there are people who have risen from far more terrible circumstances. But it was very rough at times and punctuated with loss and pain, which forced us to a point of real strength. After all, something has to shine the diamond.

## Nicole

The tendency to play the victim card is strong in our culture, particularly for women. I absolutely understand why—I think it goes back to feeling compared. A shitty childhood, or bad circumstances along the way, is one way to distinguish yourself or justify why what *might* have been never came to be. I get it. The pull to go there is strong because it's a built-in excuse—and it can also seem like a reason. I feel very fortunate that my life didn't go to a dark place, that Brie and I found the inner strength to fight against a dimmer destiny. We are strong, yes, but I also credit my grandfather, Pop Pop, for making sure that it didn't happen. I think he knew that Brie and I were right on the line of a different sort of life and he stepped in as much as he could. He made us realize that our futures could be brighter than a childhood of abuse might suggest.

And so, at a young age, Brie and I decided we did not want to be victims. Instead, we wanted to be survivors, the heroes of our own stories, to take control and responsibility for our lives. It's a fine line and hard to do—acknowledging that you have been a victim, that you have been wronged, but at the same time not letting the victimhood continue to take your life hostage. Otherwise the original crimes and original hurts just end up taking your entire life away—and we thought we had already given up enough.

Everyone has sad stories and happy stories. Unfortunately, pain is a permanent part of life, no matter how much money, or privilege, or opportunity you might have. You can't escape pain. It's the darkness contrasting all that is wonderful and bright, it's what gives life texture. So we made an unconscious decision when we were younger to process the pain as best as we were able, and then to spend the rest of our lives showing the world how strong we truly are. I think we were able to do this, in part, because we were able to draw strength and resiliency from each other, because we weren't necessarily feeling low at the exact same times. It's like those couples who say that they never got divorced because they never wanted to get divorced at the same time. We decided not to use our pain to justify falling behind—instead, we decided to use our pain to make a difference, dragging each other forward.

## Brie

It was hard to not be envious of the kids who had it easier growing up—who had more stable parents, whose homes weren't broken. But hardship has its upsides, too—in some ways, it's a great and motivating opportunity. It gives you something to press off as you hunt for something different. It makes it easy to determine exactly what you don't want to re-create. We knew we wanted something better. And we knew if that was going to happen, it was within our power to make it so.

The following pages are not promo cutting, they are reality. And while some of the storylines in the ring have not been "true," this overall through line is: We are the heroes of our own story, and our story is our own to make. While we experienced some of our stories together, a lot of it happened to us individually, and we had to go it alone—even though we are identical twins, our stories are incomparable. And your story will be incomparable, too.

# INCOMPARABLE

# CHAPTER 1

# TWIN MAGIC

## *2002-2008*

San Diego, California
Los Angeles, California
McDonough, Georgia
Tampa, Florida

## *Nicole*

I made my *SmackDown* debut on August 29, 2008, sitting in the dark, under the ring. I had snuck in during a commercial break, when all audience eyes were trained on suspended screens up high—I wore a black hooded sweatshirt pulled tight over my face. I walked into the arena in the darkness with the WWE stage managers who were transitioning the ring to the next match. Nobody noticed when I rolled below.

There was a monitor down there, so I could watch as my identical twin sister, Brie, walked the ramp to the ring. We had used all our own money—and we really didn't have any at the time—to make wrestling gear for our debut. The outfits were fine—red, basic, totally PG and unthreatening. But the veterans, in a classic hazing move, wouldn't let us wear them—because "red" was another wrestler's color. It sounds weird because WWE is such a big production you'd think they'd orchestrate every moment and choreograph the backstage, too. But in many ways they run it like a mom-and-pop operation and let wrestlers work it out themselves. At that time in particular, the veterans had all the power in the locker room. Those sorts of mind games were just part of the backstage experience, especially for the women. There was really nothing we could do but bite our lips and then hustle to come up with something else. You make and pay for your own gear in WWE, with no oversight or input from management—there's no costume closet or official wardrobe department. So we dug through our gym bags to find something that would work, which is how we ended up in black workout pants we had worn to the gym earlier that day, spray painted with glitter at the hems, and silver tankinis (the seamstresses helped us cut up some bathing suits we found in our luggage and then stitch them to our pants). Not exactly the first impression we were hoping to make, but the only thing we could come up with in a few short and panicked hours in Pittsburgh, Pennsylvania. We changed in the arena bathroom, because the veterans wouldn't let us change in the locker room. We were semi–main event, which means we were right before the main show. The appetizer.

Brie was wrestling Victoria, a talented longtime WWE veteran and former Women's Champion. She was known for her red hair and a Widow's Peak finishing move that was a neckbreaker. (Essentially, she would hoist you up, back-to-back, before dropping to her knees. It hurts.) As the two went after each other, Brie held her own with some old-school snaps and a flying snapmare before Victoria started screaming "Welcome to *SmackDown*, Brie" and "Not tonight, sweetheart." She was in Brie's face and dominating her with a lot of hair-pulling and a standing moonsault (essentially a backflip into a body slam). Below deck in the dark, I adjusted my costume, hair, and makeup to match Brie as she became more and more disheveled and out of breath. Ninety seconds in, a panting Brie crawled in to join me, while the crowd screamed: "Get back in the ring! Get back in the ring!" And then, in our first ever "Twin Magic" maneuver, Victoria grabbed me by the legs and pulled me out, tossing me back up. I pretended to be exhausted as she grabbed me by the hair, and then I flipped her over and pinned her for a three count.

So, while Brie was the first to walk the *SmackDown* ramp, I was the first to win a *SmackDown* match. I cemented my victory with a really cringe-y dance, where I jumped up and down like an overexcited contestant on *The Price Is Right*, rocked my hips back and forth, and flipped my hair. (The bump and grind wouldn't be perfected for a few years.)

## Brie

When my entrance music hit—a classic called "Feel Your Body," from the WWE music vault—I thought I might vomit. I was so scared my vision went blurry. The arena probably had close to seventeen thousand people in it, which is staggering when you're used to wrestling in church parking lots and JCCs for a few dozen die-hard fans. I didn't have a vignette or anything, because I had never been on TV before. So they announced my name and I walked out to silence. They probably assumed I was a local, because WWE will do that occasionally. (The locals they tap are actually indie wrestlers, so they're experienced in the ring and won't hurt themselves, but they'll let them have a match, where they typically get destroyed.) Randomly, Freddie Prinze Jr. was the writer who was working with me at WWE and he was a fount of positivity—he was so encouraging and just kept telling me, "You got this," on repeat, until I could say it back to him. In his non-acting life, Freddie is a crazy wrestling fan—working with him on our debut just made the whole thing even more surreal.

Fortunately, my adrenaline took over and put me on some sort of autopilot—kind of like what I would guess an out-of-body experience would feel like. I walked down the ramp and rolled into the ring. I don't remember much of that first match except that Victoria was awesome to work with. I felt terrible that she had to put me over and let me win, because that sucks for a veteran—

but she told me not to worry. Throughout the match, she really helped me out, and kept talking into my ear about what to do next: "Slow down . . . not yet . . . I'll tell you when." In recounting it, it sounds an awful lot like sex.

We were some of the first women ever to debut on the main stage as wrestlers, rather than as valets, managers, or love interests for the men. This was one of the reasons that the neck hairs of the other women in the locker room were up. The only downside of skipping straight to the fighting, and I'm not complaining here, is that when you valet, which is essentially escorting wrestlers to the mat and then working up the crowd by taunting the rival valets, you have time to get a storyline going that the crowds care about. You can draw attention and interest in a no-pressure way—you are just icing on the cake, circling the ring. Because we got to skip those steps, and in the process might be helping to set a new precedent for the women coming up behind us, we felt a lot of extra pressure to do well out there.

The audience reaction was pretty great considering we were total newcomers, and my identity as an identical twin was a secret (we wouldn't be "outed" for several months after Victoria grew suspicious in a promo backstage when I asked the seamstresses to make me two dresses . . . just in case). You want the crowd to clap, or you even want them to boo—boredom is the worst fate for any wrestler. The minute they lose interest and start checking their text messages or decide it's a good time to go to the bathroom, you're done. Because women's matches are so much shorter than the men's, typically only two minutes during

TV events, you don't have time to get their attention again to show them what you can do. So my intent was pretty simple: I wanted to be memorable, to pique the crowd's interest, and to show them that despite the fact that I was a small girl, I could still fight.

While we had the luxury of making our debut before social media was a part of daily life—and the trolling that often comes with it—we did get indications that the fans were into us. We trended #1 on Yahoo! for two days straight after our debut, which was the biggest barometer of popularity at the time. So we stayed on the main roster and weren't sent back down to FCW, WWE's developmental promotion at the time. Our debut was good enough that it made a lot of trouble for us with the other girls backstage. It was rough—like the worst kind of sorority—but we got it. You have to be able to earn your stripes as a wrestler, to know what's worth fighting about. We learned that you don't get to change in the locker room your first day out. Or your fiftieth. There are ever-changing rules about what you can wear and what moves you can do—essentially, anything perceived as someone else's signature is off-limits. It was cutthroat, and they hated us. There was a lot of bullshit, but we had decided to stick—and so we did exactly that, with smiles on our faces. When they realized that we weren't going anywhere, they started to leave us alone (more on all of that later).

After our match, we celebrated in Gorilla—the area between backstage and the ramp where you wait before you go out—with Victoria, Freddie, and Vince McMahon. It was a great moment, and everyone was really happy for us. Then we booked it to the Hyatt across the street for celebratory drinks. Because hot damn, Nicole and I had just made our debut on WWE TV.

## Nicole

I got a boob job in 2012. What can I say, I had always, always wanted big boobies, particularly since mine just disappeared after I started to get really fit for wrestling. It took me a long time to make the $6,500 to pay for them. I have never messed with my face—intentionally, that is. In 2008, weeks before our main stage debut when we were still down in Florida at FCW, I was with another wrestler looking at a magazine that we had all been featured in. He was sitting up on the apron, when another guy— whose stage name was Sweet Daddy Sanchez—hit the ropes. It ricocheted back and hit this guy, Jack Swagger, whose massive face collided with mine. He sent me flying—I literally caught air and flew several feet—and my nose just busted open. It was like being head-butted by The Rock.

Nattie Neidhart (Natalya), who was wrestling down in Florida with us at the time, rushed me to the locker room. I didn't want to tell anyone because it was hours before a match, so I mopped up the blood, iced my nose, and slathered on about two inches of foundation. I wrestled that night and then went to the trainer, who told me that not only had I shattered my nose, but I had suffered a mild concussion as well. Brie was with Craig, her boyfriend at the time, back in Los Angeles, and so another wrestler named Nic was nice enough to keep me awake all night (not like that you pervs!). The next morning, I looked like a dinosaur—you couldn't see the bridge of my nose or even my eyes. And I have a black eye on my right side to this day from stuck blood, which no doctor or dermatologist or acupuncturist has been able to fix. When we were brought up to the main roster a few weeks later, they decided to minimize my time in the ring (i.e., my face in front of an HD video camera) until my face had more time to heal—the thing about being an identical twin is that you're supposed to look identical.

## Brie

Speaking of boob jobs, I will never get one—though it had been one of the first questions from WWE when we showed up at Diva Search at the Ritz-Carlton in Marina del Rey about a year and a half earlier. "Are you open to a boob job?" We flipped out, and started to tell them off, escalating to about a 10 in just a few seconds in true Bella fashion. We had shown up that morning with a lot of excitement and definitely ready to wrestle. As soccer players—Nicole was toying with the idea of moving to Italy to play professionally before I dragged her to the audition—the idea of sports entertainment seemed made for us. We made tank tops—"Breezy Fo Sheezy" and "Nicole Fo Sho"—and put on bandanas and sneakers in anticipation of getting to fight. (We weren't worried that neither of us had ever actually been in a ring.) What we found instead was a long line of girls dressed like go-go dancers. The girl in front of us, Layla, was beautiful. She was also dressed like an athlete, and so the three of us marveled at the spectacle around us, confused and a little concerned. While she ended up going on to win Diva Search (she did *not* need a boob job), we didn't make it to the final eight. But Kristin Prouty, who worked in talent for WWE, convinced them to send us to a developmental wrestling facility in McDonough, Georgia, called Deep South. I guess she thought we had what it would take to fight in that ring and win.

## Nicole

Now, before everyone gets up in arms about the Diva Search go-go dancing casting call comment, Brie and I were Hooters girls. And once you are a Hooters girl, you are always a Hooters girl. And as a woman, I firmly believe it is every woman's prerogative to use what God gave her and screw the haters (not literally). I think we found the audition outfits troubling and the boob job comment offensive because we thought we were there as athletes. Sexy athletes, sure—but not just there to be ringside eye candy. After all, we had seen the WWE's "Attitude Era"—a time in the late 1990s to early 2000s when women were expected to fight in bras and thongs, pull each other's hair, and then make out in the ring. That time was supposed to be over, replaced by a more family-friendly WWE, where women were allowed to actually wrestle.

Our brother, JJ, who is two years younger, loved the Attitude Era. He watched wrestling all the time when he was a kid—he was obsessed particularly with The Rock and Stone Cold Steve Austin. He would follow us around and try to take us down with his finisher, which he called "The Priest." It was a gimmick where he would make the sign of the cross and then give us the "Holy Elbow," which involved him dropping his arm on our heads. He was in the fourth or fifth grade and was a little shit, so it was pretty annoying. Brie and I hadn't thought about wrestling much beyond evading JJ until we landed jobs at a California Hooters when we were eighteen.

## Brie

After high school, we both needed to get out of Arizona for different reasons (that we'll get to in a bit). So we enrolled in Grossmont Community College in San Diego. We had been born there, and we had family nearby. Our grandparents stretched to pay for our housing—at "The Conq," no less. It was a famous party dorm on the San Diego State University campus where my mom had gotten drunk a lot when she was young. ("Oh great, that's where they're putting you?" was her response when we shared the good news.) And despite our parents' divorce a few years earlier, our mom scraped together enough money to cover our first-semester tuition. But we needed cash to pay for food and books. And when you're in college, nothing brings in the dollar bills like waitressing.

It's actually hard to get a waitressing job when you're underage, because you can't serve hard alcohol. The only place that was hiring eighteen-year-olds was Hooters, since they're wine and beer only. The Mission Valley outpost was actually the highest performing franchise in the world, probably because it was right after 9/11 and we were at war. All the military guys from Camp Pendleton came hungry and often. And they were amazing tippers: God bless the military. They definitely paid for a lot of our textbooks, and, if we're honest, beers at Bennigan's after our shifts, trips to Tijuana, and ho heels. Because they didn't have much to spend their money on, they would come in straight off the ship and leave a $20 tip on a $30–$50 tab. With a menu of cheap beer and chicken wings, it's hard to get the tab north of that. And they would never skip out on the bill. (A note on waitressing: Not only does your waitress have to pay your bill if you skip, but the government assumes a 20 percent tip take-home, so if you leave less than that, she has to pay taxes on money she didn't actually make. So no, you're not actually giving a middle finger to the establishment, you're just screwing over someone who is probably living paycheck to paycheck.)

## Nicole

Working at Hooters was the best. Many of our closest friends to this day were made there. The pantyhose we had to wear are still our ride-or-die go-to in the WWE (they hold *everything* in), and we were invited to all the best parties. And unexpectedly, we always felt protected. It's funny because when we went in for our Hooters interviews, we wore multiple bras (pre–boob job, remember?), thinking that being flat-chested would be a dealbreaker. But it wasn't really like that. Plus, we had the whole twin thing going.

My first night on the job, some jerk slapped my ass so hard he left a red rooster on my butt cheek. I assumed that was just the sort of thing that happened at Hooters. I told a fellow waitress about it under my breath. "He did what?" she asked, followed by a quick "Where is he?" In under a minute, the manager and one of the line cooks had kicked him out and called the cops. A few years later, when I was a Hooters veteran and tolerated no bullshit, a bunch of Raiders football players came in to eat before playing against the Tampa Bay Buccaneers in the Super Bowl. They were rowdy, and one of the players grabbed me by the hair, bent me over, and pretended to do me doggy style. I flipped out and kicked them all out, Super Bowl be damned. You had to be a strong type of girl to work there—if it wasn't contending with ass slappers and boob grabbers, then it was dealing with people who judged your value system for putting on the tank top and serving beer in the first place. But I have never played the victim or the martyr—and I have certainly never felt compelled to ask permission to do what I want. Brie and I both learned at a young age how to take care of ourselves. And we both knew how to work the system to make some bank. I felt empowered, like I could conquer the world—and I dared any man to fuck with me without getting a fist to the face.

## Brie

As a Hooters waitress, there was one drawback, and those were the monthly pay-per-view WWE weekend matches. The guys would post up for three hours and nurse a soda and some cheese fries while they watched wrestling. Tying up a table like that without ordering a banquet is a bummer for a waitress unless you're going to compensate with a massive tip. (They didn't.) The WWE fans at the time were intense. One guy even brought his collection of troll dolls. He would arrange them in a semicircle across a four-top and blow on them for good luck. It was still the Attitude Era and the show was essentially rated R. You didn't get the young girl fans, then, and as a woman it was hard to watch even though you could tell the ladies actually knew how to wrestle. Now the young girls look at us like we're Wonder Woman. But back then, the female wrestlers weren't allowed to be heroes—it was more spectacle than sport. It made me angry that they didn't give the women the same opportunities as the men.

## Nicole

Back then, our heroes were Carla Overbeck, Brandi Chastain, and Mia Hamm, who had gone to the Olympics for soccer. I'll never forget that Mia Hamm/Michael Jordan Gatorade commercial, where they faced off in different sports: "Anything you can do, I can do better." Mia Hamm was better than any man. That was my belief system. I felt like that reality was within my grasp.

It was hard to leave Hooters, to be honest. The money was really good and we worked with all of our closest friends. They even give you benefits after you've been there for two years. And because we were all considered "entertainers," they paid $8 an hour, instead of typical waitressing hourly pay. But Brie started working with an L.A.-based modeling agency and was getting called to the city more and more. Two of our Hooters friends wanted to come with us, and so we packed the car and drove north to Los Angeles to a cramped two-bedroom on La Cienega and Olympic.

At that point, we had done a few things. We were the first World Cup twins to tour with Budweiser in California; we were promotional models at conventions; Brie was a fitting model for DC Shoes. No massive breaks, but enough affirmation that we could make some extra money while we figured out what we wanted to do with our lives.

## Brie

What we definitely wanted to do with our lives was have fun. We lived in a dump, but we all had the best time—except for Nicole, who was still involved with (and secretly married to) her high school boyfriend. The rest of us were all dating athletes, actors, people who had names—and the club scene in Los Angeles was on fire. I don't know if it's because it was before social media, but there was a freedom and lack of self-consciousness that was just so liberating. We would go, and dance, and beg for free drinks from the bartenders (bartenders will always be our weakness) until the clubs closed. Sunset would be a parking lot as we'd slowly crawl west for a late-night feast at Mel's Diner.

I saw drugs for the first time at some of those parties, but I was never interested in that. My dad has struggled with addiction, particularly when we were kids, and so I had absolutely no curiosity. Beyond smoking the occasional joint with a group of friends—and a short stint in high school as a chain cigarette smoker—I was really just a beer girl. While I've grown up to be a wine snob, at the time, if you gave me a Bud Light I was thrilled. I think that's one of the reasons people loved our group—we were just happy-go-lucky Cali girls. While our extended Hooters gang all came from broken homes and pretty unhappy childhoods, we were enjoying our liberation and excited for the next chapter. Because of that, or in spite of that, we were all relaxed and low-key. We also liked to eat, which was shocking to the guys who hung out with us. I'll never forget when one of our friends ordered the meat platter, which was essentially a side of cow. The guy she was with couldn't get over that she had not only ordered it, but intended to finish it, all by herself. "That's just for you?" he kept repeating. Meanwhile, we thought she had made a great dietary choice since it didn't have any carbs.

## Nicole

We thought we should get real jobs while we auditioned, and so our friend Jayme, who was working as an assistant for the owner of an independent music label, hooked us up with A&R jobs. While the idea of listening to music for a living sounded cool in theory, we had no idea what we were doing. We would just eat our Baja Fresh burritos for lunch and put on our headphones. One day, the owner told us that Suge Knight was going to come by and that he might shoot up the joint. We knew it was a lie, but it was a weird enough one that we got in our car and decided to never come back. We had ninety-nine problems already, and didn't need Suge Knight to be one of them. Though it was hard to imagine that he gave a shit about this particular independent music label.

I started working for Metalstorm Entertainment, who produced all the Quiksilver films. I was driving down to Oceanside every day from L.A., a commute that got really old, fast. So I ditched my sister and moved back to San Diego for my next chapter.

## Brie

After Nikki left, I decided to go back to the career I knew best. I landed a job as a waitress at Sushiya, a popular Japanese joint on Sunset. A lot of celebrities and Hollywood types would come in, which is how I met Craig. He was the guitarist for a rock band, who I went on to date for five-and-a-half years (more on that later). I also met Jay Bernstein, a producer and manager (Farah Fawcett, Sammy Davis Jr., Suzanne Somers, Michael Landon), who told me there was something special about me. Now, when you're a waitress in Los Angeles, you hear this sort of thing so often it triggers an immediate eye roll. But he convinced me to take a scholarship to Ivan Markota's acting school. I figured, "Fuck it, I'm here in L.A., why not?" It was actually an amazing experience because it was my first formal introduction to acting. It made me both ask and answer the question of whether becoming an actress was something I actually wanted. The answer was no. At first, the classes were interesting, but very quickly it came to feel like I didn't have the freedom to create in there. I was being told exactly how it needed to be done, and that didn't capture my imagination. It felt boring. I called Jay and apologized. I told him that I simply didn't want to follow a script. Acting in that way wasn't for me.

I was hanging out with Craig in the L.A. music scene. It was an incredible experience and reawakening for me. I've always been really drawn to the arts, music, painting, and poetry, but it wasn't something my parents prioritized. I craved the exposure. Art was also something that defined my high school boyfriend, Bear—in my eyes, artists were gods. In L.A. with Craig, I went to poker nights at Jerry Cantrell's house for chrissakes—Alice in Chains was one of the soundtracks to high school for me. I got to travel to Europe for the first time when Craig was touring throughout Spain. He was a much bigger star internationally, and it was incredible to watch him move an arena through music. I was blown away by his power to transfix the crowd just through his ability to perform. I wanted to be able to do that, too. I was also blown away by the groupies, who were completely enthralled with him—their fanaticism for my boyfriend freaked me out!

While Sushiya was good to me, I needed to make more money. I got a cocktailing job at the Mondrian, a particularly scene-y hotel at the time on Sunset. You could work one or two nights a week and still make your rent. I've always been one of those people who needs a cushion, which I certainly wasn't going to get from my parents. While Nicole is content to fly by the seat of her pants—she was known at the time for only having $10 in her bank account when rent was due—I'm a saver. I always prefer to live well within my means, and when you're a waitress, your means aren't high. I wanted the cushion, in part, so that I could travel with Craig when he toured. It was the first opportunity I had ever had to see the world. I've never been obsessed with owning nice things, but I wanted experiences.

## Nicole

While Brie fell deeper in love with Craig, I was in a relationship black hole with a pro snowboarder. It was a period of extreme jealousy and codependence, and I was spending a lot of time with him in Salt Lake City, where he lived near his ex-wife and kids.

We traveled a lot for his snowboarding, and our existence in general revolved around him and his career. This was much to the dismay of Brie, who felt like I was putting everything on hold for a guy who was very controlling. (Sometimes when you're in it, it's hard to see it.)

My boyfriend agreed to spend some time with me in San Diego, and so I moved back to finish community college. I walked onto the soccer team, leading the girls to a state championship and landing myself MVP in California. My coach at the time thought I was very marketable and urged me to move to Italy to try to make it as a professional player. That sounded like a great idea if I could figure out how to make it work with my guy. But then Brie's agent called her about the WWE Diva Search, and we decided to take another look at women's wrestling.

## Brie

There was no way that we weren't going to do the wrestling training program at Deep South. Back then, there were two territories for wrestlers in developmental who had come up from the independents: Deep South Wrestling in McDonough, Georgia (DSW), and Ohio Valley Wrestling in Louisville, Kentucky (OVW). (Brock Lesnar, Dave Bautista, and many others all came up through OVW.) The Deep South session was three days long, though it felt like a week. It was a valid shot at getting put into developmental, as WWE scouted the talent down there, looking for girls who could fight. It was very *Glow*, in that nobody knew what they were doing. The key difference was that we weren't all in it together—we were competing to get out of there as fast as possible. There were girls who were essentially stuck in Georgia, and they were pissed about it. They didn't really have a shot at making it into developmental, but the coaches and trainers kept them around. They needed them to wrestle and train up the newcomers. They seemed to know this and were pissed about it, but weren't willing to accept it and give up. Needless to say, they gave us a hard time. When we walked in, I remember one girl turning to her friend and saying, "Really? They don't look like models." (To be fair, at five-foot-six, I don't think we looked like supermodels either—but at the time, WWE was scouting models and trying to turn them into wrestlers.) Some of the women down there definitely refused to teach us how to take bumps, instead giving us advice that almost guaranteed we'd get hurt. But that was just part of the drill and we got it. In fact, we relished it. They had told us to spend the time watching, but we insisted on getting into the ring the first day—we wanted to be sure we'd like it as much as we thought.

*Nicole*

It was pretty brutal, but it was also love-at-first-bump for us. We just *knew* that we were meant to do this, so the bullshit from the other girls didn't really bother us. We had big smiles and lots of energy, which probably only added fuel to the fire. But that's how we operated—heads up, eyes on the prize, plenty of beer at the party for everyone. It always felt easier to show no resistance and let the girls talk shit and walk all over us, than to fight the locker room fights. We saved our energy for the ring.

And we had each other, which was huge. When the girls at Deep South wouldn't teach us much, we just tried to teach each other based on what we saw in the ring. The thing about wrestling is that when you don't know what you're doing, it hurts—those hits and falls are real, and when you haven't been trained to lessen the blow, shield your body, or fake contact, you feel it everywhere. That first night in Georgia we broke the motel room's TV and a console drawer practicing our holds. We made it look kind of right and hoped nobody would notice. The second night, we spread ice across the bed and just lay down on it. We were so sore we couldn't move.

We learned a lot in those three days about how things work. There's really no rhyme or reason to who gets signed or who doesn't, you have to just let it ride. We also learned about how you need to operate outside the ring. One of the guys down there wanted to talk about the show and work us into a gimmick, and he stopped by our hotel room one night to talk it through. So naïve, we didn't foresee that everyone couldn't stop talking about the fact that a guy was in our room, convinced that we had staged some sort of kinky threesome. We also had our first taste of kayfabe, which in wrestling is maintaining your in-ring persona outside of the ring, whenever wrestling fans are around.

Before social media, WWE was all about kayfabe: If you were a babyface in the ring, you were a babyface outside the ring; if you were a heel, you would act like a heel in public. We went to a café with some of the girls down in Deep South, and we were all in line to order food when some fans approached. Two girls had a match that weekend: They said "kayfabe" under their breath, separated, and started to give each other dirty looks. It was bizarre at times, but it was so fun!

The goal at Deep South was to get a contract. There were WWE scouts on the ground, and trainers were filming with handheld camcorders looking for talent who could move well and who might be able to hold main stage attention. At the end of our three-day trial, they told us they were interested in having us come back and train for real. (Side note: The restaurant we all ate at for a last night celebration was Hooters, proving that all roads do lead home.)

## Brie

We went back up to San Diego to talk to our family about what we were thinking. Particularly our grandfather, Pop Pop, who was the primary father figure in our lives. When we told him we wanted to become pro wrestlers and needed his blessing, he objected passionately. He wanted us to get married to nice guys and have babies, which was certainly a more assured future. He wanted to know we would be safe, tended to, protected. He always gave us good advice, and his voice was one of the only ones that actually mattered to us. So we talked a lot about how to convince him that this wouldn't be a waste of time. His knowledge of WWE was also limited to the Attitude Era, and so we understood why he wouldn't want his precious granddaughters doing bra-and-panty matches. If he had been alive to see us flourish, he would have loved it—and he would have laughed so hard.

Our grandfather passed away shortly after, on November 28, which was devastating for our entire family. We told WWE we needed time to be with our family. In that time off, they decided to shut down Deep South and began opening a new program in Tampa called FCW. They were investing in a new facility and building out a program. They offered us $500 a week and we took it gladly. When the program opened, we moved to Florida.

Craig and I had been together for two years, and we both thought we would be together forever. He was both hurt and shocked when I told him I was taking a job as a professional wrestler and moving to Florida. I felt like there was no way forward except through Tampa. If I didn't give wrestling a valid shot, I would always regret it, and so he begrudgingly helped me pack and promised to come visit. I clicked with him, but it seems I had clicked with wrestling even more. It was the first thing that I had felt passionate about in a long time, and I needed to see it through. Our relationship wasn't dramatic and we had endured distance before, so I felt like I could put it on ice while I went on this epic adventure.

## Nicole

My boyfriend was less understanding than Craig, and completely flipped out about the idea of me working around men who were dressed in little more than underwear. It was silly. I'm not a cheater, and I certainly know how to handle myself around guys, even those who are scantily clad—but he was consumed with jealousy. There was no way I was not going, though—in fact, the more someone tells me no, the more my response is "Screw you." Our relationship lasted only a few more short and horrible months.

Brie and I wanted to make an adventure out of the drive, so we sold off one of our cars for cash and packed up the more reliable Malibu with all of our possessions. We plotted out a road trip. It took us through San Antonio to see our aunt Toni and uncle Tom (and a massive rainstorm that I thought might wash the car off the road). From there, we headed to Mobile, Alabama. We were tired and hungry, and so we went downtown for burgers and beer, which seemed like an absolutely normal thing to do. We headed into the first spot we could find and grabbed seats at a four-top. And there we sat. Nobody came over to take our order. The joint was full of bikers, who were all staring—naturally, we assumed this was because we were hot, tan twins. Finally, two bikers walked over and kicked out the other two chairs at our table, leaning over to say: "Your kind is not welcome here." Surprised, we responded, "Cali girls?" Their response: "No, Mexicans." We were blown away. We didn't want to get into a fistfight, so we got up to leave. On our way out we asked the band to play "California Girls" by the Beach Boys. No clue if they obliged, because we got the fuck out of there. At the end of the block there was a jazz club with a very different clientele. We poked our heads in and asked if we could come in. We were welcomed, openly and warmly. We stayed there until late that night drinking and laughing with the locals. It would appear that there are two sides of Mobile, Alabama.

## Brie

While that night ended well, it was the first time that Nikki and I had ever experienced overt racism. Both California and Arizona are melting pots, and we were certainly not the only girls around who came from an ambiguous mixture of races and cultures (we've since done genetic reports that confirmed we are part Mexican, Italian, Native American, British, etc.). The South was a new sort of reality. Even northern Florida, surprisingly enough. In our time at FCW, we once wrestled at a boys and girls club where people in the crowds yelled, "Spic! Spic! Spic!" There were far too many Confederate flags around town for us to feel comfortable.

While the racism was deeply fucked up, it put some of the locker room bullshit into proper perspective. While we didn't have it in us to try to win over the hearts and minds of the KKK, we did feel strong enough to endure some hate from the other female wrestlers. And we understood their frustration. There had been wrestlers on the indie market for years trying to get into the developmental program, and we had cut the line. We didn't come from wrestling royalty, and we hadn't put in years wrestling abroad in the independents. But we felt strongly that even though roster sizes seem limited, our success was not an impediment to anyone else making it. The WWE is very fluid, where you can go up and down from developmental to the main roster overnight. Vince McMahon let us all be the creators of our own destiny. The fact that anyone was there meant they had a shot, too, and we weren't going to take that from them. Honestly, it felt like if there had been less attention spent on trying to pull each other off the top turnbuckle, more of us would have made it up there.

## Nicole

WWE's plan was to build out part of a canned food factory into a full-fledged FCW center. This has since happened, and it's spectacular. But its origins were far more humble. We helped put up the first two rings in there, which is wild—and those rings shared space with the canned foods. In fact, the cans became our favorite props when they taught us how to cut promos. They were all staged in either a grocery store, a gas station, or an airline thanks to the backdrop. It was also swelteringly hot and humid, as it is inclined to be in Florida in the summer. There was no AC, and while we'd roll the garage doors up to try to get some sort of cross-breeze going, we baked in there. We would change the mats four times a day because they would get so slick with sweat. It was really nasty. So nasty that Brie and I got ringworm on our cheeks. We never figured out which wrestler infected everyone else, but it's almost surprising that we didn't come down with worse. It was a swamp of wrestling sweat.

When we arrived, the canned food factory wasn't yet a reality and so they had two rings set up at a batting cage frequented by all the local Little Leaguers. It didn't dampen how amazing the scene was. We acted like rabid WWE fans, jaws on the floor, when we first walked in. We had never seen advanced wrestling live before, and we bought every bump they threw. Steve Kern, one of the coaches, turned to the other coach, Dr. Tom Prichard, and said: "Tom, I think they think this is real."

They put us right into the fire and asked the other girls to go at us hard and throw us around until we learned how to take the hits and fall right. The girls certainly obliged. We learned how to tuck our chins and land in certain ways to lessen the impact—when you don't know what you're doing, you feel all of it, and it kills. But we loved it. Because we knew we were really green and had so much to learn, we attended night classes to try to get better. Tom gave us a lot of extra attention because we were so eager. It's funny, because he is such a big, manly wrestler, but he's the one who came up with the backflip into the ring and the Bella booty shake. Who would have guessed? I picked our entrance music, though—"I'mma Shine," by Youngbloodz—not realizing that the lyrics were about strippers. I thought they were so uplifting! I was thinking, "I'm going to shine out there!"

All in, we were wrestling for eight to ten hours a day. We'd take a short break before night school to nap. We'd get up early in the morning to power walk with bands and Saran Wrap tight around our waists before wrestling (don't ask, not a good idea, but we thought it would help us shed water weight fast). Other than that it was eating, wrestling, and sleeping. We were intent on making it: Physical storytelling—using our bodies to portray fear, anger, pain, triumph—felt like what we had always been meant to do.

About two months in, we had our first match. Brie and I took on Krissy Vaine and Nattie, and we beat them. Or, to be more precise, they put us over. The thing about developmental is that the matches are amazing. For one, everyone is trying to get to the main roster, and you can feel that desire in the way all the women fight. But more important, we weren't limited by time the way you are in live and TV events, when women typically only get about two minutes per match at the time. There also weren't expectations that we'd pull each other's hair—spectacles that are still part of main stage fights. Instead, it was pretty straightforward wrestling. But instead of performing in front of arena crowds, we went at each other in church parking lots and high school auditoriums where there *might* be a dozen people in the stands.

All in, we spent fourteen months in developmental, and I'm grateful for every minute that we had. Getting to the main stage is all about timing. Some girls moved up in two months because the WWE creative team felt like a male wrestler needed a valet or manager and wanted a specific look. But we were happy to stick around at FCW for as long as they would have us and really learn how to wrestle. Once you're on the main roster and on the road all week, you don't really get a chance to train. Instead, you learn through matches, and those matches are short.

The other upside of staying in developmental is that there wasn't TV time down there yet (now it's a massive production), and so we got to stay under the radar. There was also no social media, so there was no pressure to build a massive following. At best, you would make fliers and pass them out for shows. We didn't even have Facebook profiles. Nobody had any idea that there were twins down in developmental. Wild to think about now.

While we both would have loved to assume we could make it to the main roster on our own as solo performers, our pull was in our twindom, as had been the case throughout our lives. More specifically, our power source was the fact that we were identical. Kind of. When we started at FCW, Brie weighed 117 pounds— she was essentially like a baby deer and looked like she could be snapped in two when she was up against some of the stronger women. I hadn't weighed 117 pounds in more than a decade, partly because my boyfriend liked me as thick as possible. (And I loved that.)

We were both put on diets—let's just say that Brie's was more fun than mine—until we looked more alike than we had in years. That is, we looked alike until my nose was flattened into my face. At that point, WWE had already put the gears in motion to bring us up to the main roster, so they went back to the drawing board. They came up with the idea of "Twin Magic"—i.e., keeping me under the stage until the end of Brie's matches so I could come out refreshed and win. While I've never been inclined to hang back, the chance to debut as wrestlers, rather than on the arm of one of the dudes, wasn't something I was going to turn down. Plus, as the older sister by sixteen minutes, I thought it might be time to let Brie go first.

# CHAPTER 2

# LEARNING TO FIGHT

## Nicole

Legend has it that I drop-kicked Brie into my mom's rib cage so I could make my grand entrance a full sixteen minutes before her. But I think Brie hung back on purpose—she's always been more of a homebody, more reserved—to let me test the waters.

My parents met when they were in high school—after my dad had already managed to father a kid at sixteen (he didn't find out about our sibling until after we were born). He's Mexican and dashing, and he also came from a really messed-up background. My mom was completely in love with him, which was at odds with her parents, who were strict and Catholic. It was a potent combination, and a story as old as time. Brie and I came blasting into the world when my mom was just nineteen, her freshman year at the University of San Diego. When my mom left for college, my dad, who didn't go to school, followed her and took a job as a busser at a restaurant called Milton's off Del Mar Heights (it's still there). We were born on November 21, a full month early. If I had to guess, I'd say we were conceived on Valentine's Day.

Because of my mother's "state," my grandparents felt it best that she leave college and take up residence in a girls' home in Mission Hills. There she would have the company and communion of other girls in similar straits. Hopefully, they'd be protected from the judgment and gossip of their Catholic peers. The health care she received during her pregnancy was really basic. Her insurance didn't cover ultrasounds, so the doctor just listened for a heartbeat during checkups. She was massive—really huge—but the doctor never thought to listen for a second baby. He just assumed she was having a very healthy boy.

My mom wasn't allowed to have much contact with my dad when she was at the home. Visits were only allowed occasionally, so they wrote each other a lot of love letters. My mom doesn't talk about it much, but I'm guessing it was really romantic—the forced separation, my mom in dire straits, this incoming family that they would need to provide for—and my grandfather was insistent that my mom not marry my dad under duress. He wanted to be sure that it would be a choice of love and something that my mom really wanted, not something she was forced into just because they had a kid. My grandfather knew a bit about my dad's background—my dad is the sort of person who is always preceded by his reputation—and so my grandfather had always been compassionately wary of him. When my dad was expelled from high school for fighting, my grandfather had stepped in and advocated on my dad's behalf, arguing that he was a troubled boy who needed the structure of a place to go and the backbone of an education. They took my dad back in. So he cared, but he might not have cared to have him as a son-in-law necessarily.

When my mom went into labor, I came out at 5 pounds. They cut the umbilical cord, not realizing that Brie was still up there, breeched in my mom's ribs, which immediately put her life in peril. It was many, many minutes later that a very wise nurse realized there was another heartbeat and in a panic instructed my mom to push. "Nope, I'm not pushing" was her response, which is so our mother. She can be mad stubborn. Brie came out at 4.8 pounds, not breathing, because without the umbilical cord, she hadn't been getting any oxygen.

But Brie was not about to go down that easy. After they resuscitated her, they put her in an incubator, and tucked me in there alongside her, to help her heart keep beating. My dad went out to the waiting room to tell my Nana that not only did she finally get her first granddaughter, but she got two. It was a huge shock to everyone, though in looking at photos of my pregnant mother, I'm not sure how anyone was surprised. I guess it was before the days when IVF became so common, and twins were a rarity. As my mom tells it, we attracted attention everywhere we went—particularly because we liked to hold hands, even when we were tiny babies.

## Brie

We went home from the hospital on Thanksgiving Day, and then my mom drove us straight to our grandparents' house in Phoenix. My mom had just turned nineteen and she desperately needed the help. The prospect of mothering one kid when she was still a kid herself had seemed overwhelming, but twins were impossible. My grandparents were very hands-on, more like parents than grandparents really. They were incredibly gracious about helping and ensuring that we had the best chance at thriving. Ultimately, our parents ended up getting married a year and a half after we were born.

We come from a produce farming family. Our grandfather was first generation from Italy and manned a produce store on South Street in Philadelphia. He and his four brothers moved west after World War II, because the land was cheap and it seemed like a great opportunity—they became some of the first farmers in Southern California. They started an operation called the Colace Brothers, which ultimately became Five Crowns, and then Majesty. Throughout our early childhood, our parents were itinerant, moving from Phoenix to Brawley, California, where the crops are located. Then back to Phoenix, rinse and repeat. My dad was going to school to become a sheet metal mechanic so that he could install ductwork for ACs, while my mom went to work when we were three months old, at a women's clothing boutique in El Centro called Cinderella. None of it was very stable.

The way we lived throughout our childhood probably goes a long way toward explaining why both Nicole and I desperately crave having a real home yet cannot stay rooted in any house for long.

My dad's childhood was terrible, the stuff of cautionary tales. When he was one, his dad, who was working two jobs to support the family, fell asleep on Highway 5 in California and went off the road and died. They were living on the Tijuana border at the time, and his mom, who was a heroin addict, felt overwhelmed by the responsibility, ditched her kids without telling anyone, and ran away. Our dad's grandmother found them days later—a one-year-old and a three-year-old—sitting on the table. My dad's older brother was feeding him.

When my dad was thirteen, he was in the hospital with a broken arm. He was waiting and waiting for his grandmother, the only woman who had ever really loved or mothered him, to come. A nurse walked into the room to tell him that she had just dropped dead. There was no ceremony, no emotion. Nobody knew where to send the boys until an aunt and uncle agreed to take them in. Despite the open doors, it wasn't a home filled with love. He was never allowed to mourn his grandmother, there was no tenderness where he landed.

When he started dating my mom in high school, our grandfather recognized his pain—this poor kid who had only ever known tragedy, hardness, and loss. My Pop Pop could sense how awful it had been for him, but I think he also knew that there were limits to what he, or my mom, could do to really heal those wounds. I'm sure my mom, who is warm and competent and had only ever known the assurance of a loving and stable home, thought she was up for it. She could nurture him to a place of safety and love. I think we all have that hubris when we're young, that desire to save, and that belief that we can. Obviously, it was beyond my mom's capacity, particularly at the age of twenty. When we were young, our dad would cry about his grandmother—it was hard to feel sympathy, to soften toward him, to accept any of his apparent pain and grief as an excuse for the fact that he then passed all of his hurt onto us. It felt like one more way that he was trying to share responsibility for his violent behavior, by making his grief something we needed to share. But on the flip side, we knew he was a deeply pained and hurt man.

## Nicole

I'm not one to ever argue with fate, and I can't say that I'm mad that I'm here. But our parents were kids who hadn't worked through their own childhood baggage—and they definitely weren't ready to shepherd us through ours. It would be putting it nicely to say that they were ill-equipped. My parents were so young when they had us that they named me after their favorite babysitters from childhood—one was named Nicole, the other was Stephanie. They didn't like how Nicole Stephanie sounded, so they named me Stephanie Nicole, after my dad's favorite babysitters, and then referred to me as Nicole. Only my soccer team ever called me Stephanie.

Our childhood was tough, and on the whole, our house was unhappy. This was the eighties and early nineties, when some people still spanked their kids. A lot of what happened to us was borderline acceptable—hotly debated but not officially labeled as abuse; it was certainly not nearly as stigmatized as it is now. As we grew older and started going to friends' houses for playdates and sleepovers, the difference between our own home and how our friends were raised became starker.

Our parents fought all the time—they told us that they fought like that because they loved each other. It has taken many, many years, and a ton of expensive therapy, for both of us to begin to separate fighting and love, to realize that they do not coexist to that extent in healthy relationships. We never knew what would cause our dad to fly off the handle—it wouldn't take much, sometimes just a day that was too hot—but he would get worked up and angry to the point of blacking out. Our dad had a lock on our mom's heart, and if I were to guess, I'm sure she felt responsible for some of the pain that he had endured as a kid. She didn't want to pile on with more loss and abandonment. I believe she still thought that she could save him, that we would all be enough to heal his heart. I don't think she realized that she was letting him sink the whole lifeboat in the process, with the three of us kids in there, too. He had a terrible temper, and was almost constantly angry and scary. There was too much fighting—sometimes physical—and our dad used drugs. It was too much for our house to ever feel stable. It is very clear now, starkly clear, that the only person who could save him was my dad himself, but he operated unconsciously—he never showed remorse afterward, never really cracked enough to create a conversation about whether there was a better way to be.

There were a lot of hope spots, too. These kept us all cling-ing to a fantasy that it could get better, that we could be a happy family. My parents would host these parties—they loved having people over to watch boxing, for example—and everything at our house would seem so fun, just for that night, before something would set our dad off again. They also did a lot of stuff for us together, like they would both come to our ballet classes or soc-cer practices, which always made us feel like we were a little normal or even indulged. Most kids only had one parent pres-ent, if that. We had two! They never missed a game! Our father would cook dinner, or pick us up if we needed him to, and he was fiercely but not overly protective, in a way that would make us feel loved, guarded, and cherished. But ultimately, his mood could all change in an instant. There was no rhyme or reason, and we spent our childhood walking on eggshells, hoping we wouldn't step on a land mine. There were a lot of conversations between me and Brie that went something like this: "Gosh, does Dad love us at all? Is this what it's supposed to feel like?"

## Brie

The yelling and fighting and door slamming was a constant soundtrack in our house. I think our soccer coaches knew what was going on, but I often wonder if anyone else was aware of how turbulent our home life was. Nicole and I would put up a front that we were strong, but inside we had imploded. We had no confidence, we were terrified. It sort of felt like we were living a double life. In front of my grandparents, we pretended like our home life was perfect, wholesome, and complete. I think they knew that it was actually broken, that we were being hurt by our dad, and that it was all very toxic. I think that's why they insisted on playing such significant roles in our childhood and having such a heavy influence.

Every summer, all my aunts and uncles and cousins would go and stay with Nana and Pop Pop in Lake Tahoe. It was the best time ever—a profound relief from home. We could be with people we loved without fear of setting them off or facing retribution for some small and invisible infraction. My grandparents had a condo next to the Hyatt, and we would spend a lot of our time there, trying to make a quick buck (always). When we were in fifth grade, we put out a tip bucket in front of the gift shop and danced around modeling sunglasses (our idea, not theirs). We asked the umbrella guys on the beach if they would let us be their umbrella girl assistants for scavenged tips (they obliged). We also pilfered Hyatt lotions and shampoos and tried to sell them on the beach. We made friends with all the tourists who came from Chicago, New York, and Texas, and we learned all about their lives. And I had my first make-out session, with a cute boy from San Jose, there one summer. We went to the arcade and won tickets for stuffed animals; we went out on my uncle's boat. It was like the best summer camp ever: We were allowed to run free with our cousins within a safe and contained environment. I think that's why we turned out how we did—being in that environment made us want to be better. We became aware that things could feel safer and healthier and quieter. Our grandparents' love was profound and stable and everything that we ultimately wanted in our own lives. Summers were always a period of peace that we could look forward to. They taught us to look for sanctuary back home, too, even if it was in walks to church, just the two of us. We joined the choir, because we knew it would be orderly and calm and we would be around good people.

When you grow up how we did, you equate love and pain. That chased Nicole in particular through most of her early relationships. She didn't know how to accept love and affection unless it also hurt. My mom was thoroughly under my dad's spell throughout our childhood. I don't think she can fathom how she let it happen except the belief that she could pull my dad through, that it would somehow change, that it was better to all be together than apart. I don't think that she realized that she was actually teaching us that love can feel conditional and unreliable—that she was creating a foundation for us that was unstable and full of cracks rather than the bedrock that we so desperately craved.

To this day, Nicole and I can transition from full-expletive meltdowns to peaceful dinner invitations. It has been up to people like my husband, Bryan, to show us that it's not "normal" or maintainable to act like that. And honestly, he has the patience of a saint. It has required a lot of therapy. People have had to bring awareness of our behavior to us, because like our dad, we can almost go unconscious in moments of rage and not even remember what we said. Understanding how to react without feeling overwhelming and immediate rage; practicing emotional containment instead of ramping to an extreme reaction—it is tough stuff.

It is probably ironic that we fight for a living. But part of the process has been transmuting the pain of our childhood into something productive. We prove to ourselves and others that it's possible to get up again—that you can defend yourself, you can move through a whole spectrum of emotions while simultaneously supporting those who are in battle with you. Wrestling is not a winner-take-all proposition—it is much more complicated than that. And so, too, is our relationship with our dad. It is possible to not want a lot to do with him, while still loving him from afar. It is possible to wish our childhood had been different, while also being thankful that it turned us into the women we have become.

I think that when you feel victimized, it is difficult if not impossible not to feel like you should shoulder some of the blame. That you inspired it, that you deserved it, that you participated in some way. Nicole and I have worked really hard to refuse to pick up that mantle, in all ways. We don't want to be known as victims, ever; and we certainly don't want to act like victims either. When you accept victimhood, then you are effectively letting the abuse happen again and again in real time. It is a subtle but important thing. You have a responsibility to yourself to process and work through the pain, which is very different from taking on the responsibility of it happening in the first place. We have done a lot of work to let go of the anger and to only use it as motivation, never as an excuse.

## Nicole

I always wanted to be an entertainer—and have been pursuing it since I was young. I wanted to be a supermodel, like Naomi Campbell and Cindy Crawford—it never occurred to me that I was at an extreme height disadvantage. I never believed that there were any limits, which is pretty great in retrospect. When our parents' friends came over, we'd arrange them in the living room and dress up as Posh and Sporty Spice and sing "Wannabe," a big hit at the time ("Tell me what you want, what you really, really want"). In retrospect, this was probably mortifying for our mother, but we didn't understand the lyrics—we were only in it for the audience.

At school, I was very active in drama and would always raise my hand for roles in these short films we would make as classroom projects. I always picked the ones where someone got killed, like *Jawbreakers*. At one point, as I was licking barbecue sauce off a long knife with a lot of enthusiasm, my teacher looked at me and said, "Can we talk after class?" The teachers knew what was going on, and I think my apparent relish for violence made them nervous—it's easy to understand how they thought that we would be going down a darker path. But I really just enjoyed acting, not because it was evidence of homicidal motives. For what it's worth, I also aced the monologue from *Clueless* where Cher debates Amber about the refugee crisis.

I liked the attention, and I liked to be looked at. Until a couple classmates my freshman year did something terrible. It was lunchtime, and we were all hanging out in the cafeteria. I was wearing a skirt and a thong, and they took a photo up my skirt. I remember walking into school a few days later and everyone was staring at me; by third period, a guy friend pulled me aside. "These two kids took a photo up your skirt and they're passing copies of it around."

It was horrible—the whole idea was invasive and mortifying on its own, but the photo was also distorted, and I had an ingrown hair on the bottom of my butt cheek which looked massive and red because of the angle. I felt so violated, so humiliated. The principal got involved and put the two freshmen into detention; I was close to a bunch of senior guys who tried to beat them up in there. And then my dad showed up—he threatened to kill the boys and their families and had to be restrained by cops, adding to the drama and embarrassment. I locked myself in my room and refused to come out for days.

That was the first bad sexual thing that had ever happened to me. I remember thinking, "Why did they choose me? Why did they need to humiliate me in particular? Was I asking for it?" There are no good answers to questions like that, and it's a major problem with our culture that women are always asking them. It was just a fucked-up thing to do. A prank from some dumb boys who hadn't been taught any better. A few weeks later, I wanted to walk home by myself. I think I was still struggling from the photo episode, and Brie had volleyball practice. I told my friends I was sick so they would leave me alone.

I was walking on the sidewalk when an old Cadillac came so close it actually grazed my leg. The person who was driving it was moving at a crawling pace, but it still shocked me and I jumped back. I looked over and saw a guy in a trucker hat through the open window, and he was jacking off as he tried to grab me with his other hand. And then he yelled: "Get inside and suck my dick!" I started sprinting for a neighbor's house, and he floored it. He did the same thing a week later to a fourth-grade boy and was arrested. We found out that he actually lived in our neighborhood.

*Brie*

That wasn't the last drama of our freshman year. We were also stalked by a guy in a pickup truck. He followed Nicole and me home from school one day, and we jumped some walls to escape him. Later, he parked near our house—and we could tell that he was touching himself because of the weird faces he was making. It was a sad realization to have to come to when you're fourteen years old. We told our dad, who must have alerted the neighborhood, because later that week I was standing in the kitchen when the landline rang. It was my dad, and he said: "Brie, the guy is parked down the street—I want you to go and lock the door right now." It suddenly felt like the front door was five hundred miles away as I raced to latch it, like in a bad horror movie. My dad called the cops and they arrested the guy—it turned out that he lived an hour away. I'm not sure how he found us, or why he picked us as his targets, but these incidents were some of the first times I realized that strangers could be malevolent.

Bryan always gives me a hard time for being freaked out about being alone at night, but I think most women understand why it is justified to feel scared. Even though I know how to fight and could theoretically protect myself, someone could have a gun. And, like I said, I learned, at a young age, that the world is full of creeps. Nicole and I just decided that we should assume everyone is a serial killer. I remember one night, Nicole and our friend Julia and I were walking home after a shift at Hooters, to the cute apartment that we all shared in San Diego. We were walking up to our building when a man came running out—and our neighbor from upstairs came running after him. It turned out that that guy had been in our apartment, sitting on our couch holding our underwear. And it wasn't the first time he had been there, because that same upstairs neighbor told us he had seen him coming out of our apartment before. The world is apparently full of weirdos. For that reason, even though Nicole and I have been perfectly capable of getting wild, we've always been really careful about going home with strangers or walking alone late at night. You can never be too safe.

The Christmas of our sophomore year, our dad had told us that he was going on some sort of spiritual soul journey—a trip to find himself. My mom bought him presents for this soul journey, and wrapped them, and put them under the tree. After we opened gifts on Christmas morning, he bounced. We later found out that this Christmas soul journey took place on a cruise with another woman.

## *Nicole*

My mom couldn't keep it from us—she dropped to her knees on the kitchen floor, crying and crying. What was worse, the woman he was having an affair with was the team mom from my brother's Little League team. This made it more embarrassing, more hurtful, and more problematic for all of us. Her parents called my mom, I think, because they didn't want JJ and their grandson to be affected, for it to become the talk of the neighborhood. Ultimately, it did anyway.

My dad was never faithful, and from what I recall, my parents separated a couple of times over the years. We visited him in some sort of apartment where he was living while he waited for my mom to take him back. And she always did, even though he cheated constantly and she usually heard about it. My mom is a great woman, and she was beloved throughout our community. When people knew that my dad was up to something, they always told her. They just cared about her too much. And I'm sure they thought that she would finally be ready to leave. But she was really, really taken with him—addicted in some ways. And I think she was terrified by the possibility of creating a broken home. For whatever reason, I think she believed that an unhappy home was a better alternative for the five of us than divorce. She thought that my dad had been the victim of that sort of drift and she would be subjecting us to a similar fate. On that point, she was wrong.

## Brie

After the Christmas cruise, my dad stayed away from the family for a while. Then he popped back up again and wanted to come home and pretend like everything was normal. I'm not sure how he persuaded my mom, but she let him back in. Nicole and I were furious and would have nothing to do with him, much less continue with the charade that we were a normal family. Our refusal to talk to him only enraged him more because he felt like we were disrespecting his authority. Right before Spring Break we got into a massive fight. Nicole was grounded and decided to put the time to good use and get some sun by the pool. She went to lay out in her pink bikini, which was when my parents, already upset that she wasn't in her room, noticed that she had gotten a tattoo. We actually both had, in a rebellious fit, a few weeks before. The fight quickly escalated and both of my parents followed Nicole into her room. From what I recall, my mom got in Nicole's face and Nicole pushed her back; my dad hit Nicole in the face and she fell into the curtains, while I jumped on his back to stop him. He picked us both up and threw us out of the house. Both of my parents were responsible for that. I was in pajamas. I don't think either of us was wearing shoes. We went to our friend Tammy's house and crashed with her for a few days, until her parents got suspicious and called my mom.

She told us they were coming to get us and we called our friend Arielle, the only sixteen-year-old girl we knew who could drive, and then Nicole and I tried to run. Tammy's stepdad grabbed us as we made for the door, and Nicole karate chopped his arm and booked it through the rain into the darkness—he just yelled after her in French. Nicole jumped in Arielle's pickup and took off into the night. But ever the runt, I couldn't get free.

My dad was convinced that we were on drugs. As I told him that day, I wasn't dumb, and I had no intention of being like him in any way. Save for a little bit of pot, I've never really touched the stuff. They took me to get drug tested anyway because my dad wouldn't let it go—I think he was eager to project his own stuff onto us, to find someone else to blame for his scary behavior.

Then my parents put me under their version of house arrest, minus the electric anklet. I was a smart kid, and I stashed a phone under my bed so I could call and check in on Nicole and leave money out for her.

# *Nicole*

Ironically, that week that I spent as a runaway was actually the first time I saw hard drugs. It was Spring Break, and so there were parties at parent-vacated homes every night. After most kids would head home for curfew, I'd stay behind and crash out. Late into the night, kids were doing crack, really hard drugs. It was terrifying to see and really sad, but I had nowhere else to go.

The cops kept calling my phone and leaving me messages that if I didn't come in, they'd arrest me. So I finally showed up at the station. My parents had told them that I ran away because I was on drugs, so they drug tested me. I told them my story, and asked them to call the school, to have them vouch for my dad's history of getting physical with us. And I had taken a photo of my face after he had hit me. Teachers and security guards at the school had seen things over the years—once, my dad and I got into it when he was dropping me off, and he threw a box of Kleenex at my head. A security guard came up to the truck and got in my dad's face about it. I told the cops I would rather go to juvi than go home to live with my dad again, and they believed me.

My mom realized it was over. She needed to kick my dad out of the house so I could come home, though she was still upset that I had made the decision for her. I came home and immediately started throwing all of my dad's shit into the driveway. It's really hard for my mom to talk about; I think when you are abused, you lose your head a little bit—it happens to strong and smart women all the time. They stay because they think maybe it will get better, or they're too scared to walk away because they fear the retribution will be worse. The pervasive theme is that they don't feel like they can tell anyone, because maybe they won't be believed. Police intervention was the wake-up call that my mom needed to choose our health and safety over my dad. My mom was devastated. I don't think she was truly upset with us, but I do think she was blown away that it had escalated to that point—that she had let it unfold for so many years without doing anything to make it stop. As our family secret blew open, she almost couldn't believe it herself, as much as she knew it was all true.

The four of us have recovered from those hard years, though, and have an incredibly strong bond. We know our mom would move mountains for us, and we have endless respect for her business acumen and insight (even though it's the only thing she wants to talk about).

## Brie

We were really close to my Nana and Pop Pop, and it was always tempting to go to them and tell them what was happening inside our family. It would have been so comforting to be able to confide in them, and to have their protection. At the same time, we couldn't bear the idea of how painful the full story would be to them. I think they were always concerned that things might not be okay behind closed doors, but we all always managed to put on brave faces. We reassured them that we were, in fact, just great. That's just how Nicole and I are. We don't want sympathy, we don't want people to worry or feel sorry for us. We want our connections with other people to be real, and not based on them feeling bad. Plus, we have always been inclined to put the needs of others before our own. If our grandparents had known, they wouldn't have been able to sleep at night.

After my dad finally left, we tried to establish a new normal—and my mom started going out a lot with her friends. I think it was her first chance to be young. She had been forced to skip that phase because she had us when she was just a teenager. She also seemed happy and relieved, like an unburdened version of herself. She started to date a guy who was the opposite of my dad—he drove a motorcycle, but that was the extent of his edge. He was sweet and quiet and very sensitive. He owned his own company and had his life together. It was really nice for us to see her with a guy who deserved her.

We were struggling financially, so we ultimately had to move into a smaller house. It was really cute, maybe sixteen hundred square feet or so. It only had three bedrooms, so Nicole and I shared a room again, and I shared the master bath with my mom. The backyard had a mini pool that consumed the entire space (a necessity during Arizona summers), and the living room was really cozy. My dad had always insisted on having this heavy, Western furniture. My mom's first go at decorating on her own was so much softer and more feminine. It really felt like a home. When Nicole and I moved to Tampa for FCW, we ended up taking all that furniture with us, because my mom married her boyfriend and moved in with him.

My dad really struggled—he wasn't always pleasant, he wasn't always nice, and he made it really hard. There definitely were good times—but there were more hard times. When you're a kid, the bad outweighs the good. It's so traumatizing when you're little—those memories are really tough to shake. As an adult, you're much more equipped to be able to brush off the tough stuff. When you're a kid, it sticks.

I don't think my dad ever even went to rehab—he just gave up drugs on his own. Throughout our life, I never really knew if he was controlled by an addiction or just had a strong preference for drugs. He clearly really enjoyed them, but he also seemed capable of cutting them out and going cold turkey. I didn't really know. That assessment might not be giving addiction the power and credit it deserves. It could have been more of a struggle, but to me, it always felt like it was a choice. Drugs offered a path that was easier than being responsible for his family, and so he just chose drugs instead. As a kid, I had no concept of what he was up to. He didn't seem enslaved, just angry and hurt. From what Bryan tells me, my husband's childhood seems different. His dad was ruled by alcohol. He would have done anything to liberate himself from addiction, but he couldn't stay sober.

I spent a lot of my life being really angry at my dad. In some ways, I was enslaved by the pain of my childhood. I told myself I didn't want to engage with him or go there. I just didn't have the energy to deal with all that he brings. I think the real reason, though, was that he never owned his part. He never took accountability for what he did to our family or acknowledged that he created a lot of pain. When you're the one who felt that pain, that is incredibly frustrating. It feels victimizing and disempowering. I just didn't want to go to the mat with him to try to make him own his behavior.

When Birdie was about one, my dad reached out. He drove to San Diego to meet her, and we had an incredibly moving conversation. My dad is fifty-two now and has other kids—a daughter who is older than Nicole and me, and also two young ones—a six-year-old and a two-year-old. When I saw my dad again, it was clear that he has changed profoundly. His new kids are having a far different childhood than we did.

When we sat down to talk, my dad was beyond the denial phase—he owned everything. He acknowledged how ill-equipped he had been. He had been doing the best he could with what little he had, and he admitted that he had offloaded his pain on us in a way that was unfair and unforgivable. I was able to release all the anger and hate I felt for him and to grieve our relationship so I could forgive him. I realized that the pain had been a horrible burden to carry. Even though I'd pretended like I hadn't really cared, the anger and hate had been binding me to the trauma. It was revictimizing me. It wasn't healthy. I also knew that if I want to model good relationships for Birdie, I have to learn how to have these hard conversations. I have to process what comes up for me without just shutting down. If someday Birdie and Bryan were to fight, I wouldn't want her to think it was okay to shut the door on him because I shut the door on my own dad. My dad and I are in a process of deep recovery. We're letting all the negativity go and finding a path to having a real relationship. I'm finding a way to celebrate all of his good qualities, like the fact that he is an incredibly hard worker—he works at a solar farm, and every week he drives six hours to spend time with his family. He has always been like that, always worked tirelessly.

Now that I'm a mom, I understand the concept of unconditional love—how deep and basic and profound it is. I know my dad loves me, and I know he always loved me. I didn't always feel it as a kid, but there's no version of life where loving someone means that you'll never screw up. I just don't think he could help it. He wasn't prepared to be a good dad, he'd never had a model of how it can be done. I'm gratified that he is doing so much better, that he is now at peace, and that despite it all, Nicole and I have turned out well. For better or for worse, he taught us how to fight—and he certainly knew how.

# CHAPTER 3

# BEAR

## 2001-2002

Scottsdale, Arizona

### *Brie*

It was toward the end of summer up in Bear's attic. It was late at night, a testament to the fact that neither of us had school the next day. Bear sat on a stool in front of me, all six-foot-one of him, and held a canvas, swirling paint and dabbing it here and there. He had shaggy blond hair, full lips. He was painting my portrait, and for the first time ever, it felt like I was actually being seen. His real name was Edward, but everyone who knew him called him Bear. Everyone who knew him loved him. He was just one of those people—wise beyond his years, kind, calm, prophetic. He was beautiful.

Nicole and I went to Chapparal High, a big public school in Scottsdale, Arizona. We were both good soccer players—Nicole was particularly talented, which I'll let her tell you about—though I hated the game and had been forced by my parents to play it since I was a kid. It held no joy for me, but my parents believed that good kids played sports, and so doing something else was not an option.

I was a reasonably popular girl in high school though I didn't really care either way, and I didn't associate with any specific group. My best friend Katie and I floated around, hanging out with the skater boys one day, the drama kids the next—honestly, Chili Cheese Fritos and Dr Peppers were the only constants. I never really felt a strong urge to "belong," I think probably because I always had my sister to turn to, a constant reminder of myself. She hung out with the cool kids at the ramada, one of those buildings without walls where we'd all take shelter from the hot Arizona sun. I spent plenty of time with Nicole at home, so at school I primarily hung out with my sidekick, Katie.

My sister and I were part of a church youth group, where I became close to two people in a pretty unlikely way. We were on our way to a retreat and were packed into a school bus. It was a rowdy crowd of high school juniors, even though we were all supposed to be devout Catholics. Nicole went to the bathroom and didn't return for a while, so I walked to the back to investigate. She was screaming through the door that someone had locked her inside. Nicole and I have really aggressive and quick tempers—and so I rounded on the two people sitting across from the door accusing them of pranking my sister. They looked at me like I was nuts while I continued to yell at them for being messed-up assholes. And then my sister figured out how to work the door and stepped out like nothing had happened. Typical Nicole.

Despite our aggressive introduction, Jason and Elizabeth became close friends. They went to a private school, St. Mary's. Katie and I started hanging out with them so much it would have been easy to assume we went to St. Mary's, too. (Katie even ended up dating Jason, who became her high school sweetheart.)

A few months later, Jason and Elizabeth took us to a party. I was nervous when I walked in because it was a sea of people I didn't know. Nicole is far more extroverted than I am, and really easy in a crowd—she's kind of my social beard in strange situations. When she's not around, I tend to keep to myself and find the nearest corner. Katie and I walked outside and I saw a guy at the end of the table. He was wearing a baseball T-shirt with yellow sleeves and he was clearly a skater (my weakness), and a really handsome one at that. The light hit him in a certain way, though he was one of those guys who would shine in the dark— just a star, able to draw attention in a low-key way. It was hard not to stare.

Bear was a smart-ass, and he teased me all night in a way that would be easy to mistake for flirting. We didn't exchange numbers. I left that night so bummed that he didn't ask. But by that point, everything had become about St. Mary's—I totally skipped out on the Chapparal High crew—and we started running into each other all the time at parties. There was a big kegger one night, and kids from across town were going to be there. I knew

Bear would be there, too. I was really excited to see him, but a fight broke out between the two high school boy groups over something stupid, and the whole crowd dispersed. We ended up back at Katie's, and somehow Bear found his way there.

Our parents got divorced when we were fifteen, though they had been on and off for years. When they decided to make it official, everything went sideways, and they kicked us out of the house. Nicole was considered a runaway for a week and wouldn't go back home until my mom agreed to fully kick my dad out. One of the things that had precipitated running away was the fact that Nicole and I had decided to get our first tattoos—I got a fairy on my ass because I thought of myself as a free spirit, and Nicole got a heart on fire. They were regrettable, but in that moment they felt like the only way to rebel.

I showed Bear my ass tattoo that night and then his friends dragged him away. As he was getting in the car, he finally asked for my number—he didn't have a pen but promised he had a good memory. He told me later that the guys in the car kept trying to mess him up as he repeated my number again and again.

He called me the next day and we spoke for four hours, in that way that you do when you're seventeen and you want to know absolutely everything about someone. We talked until we fell asleep on the phone. He told me his favorite color was purple, which I thought was unexpected for a dude. I told him my life story. We talked about our siblings. He had lost his oldest brother, a family tragedy that hadn't seemed to derail his sense of peace and justice. Bear was the baby, the youngest of six kids.

From that day on, we were inseparable. We had to see each other every day, and we talked all the time, locking up our home phones for hours. We had a profound connection, like we had known each other forever, like it wasn't our first rodeo. He also had a beautiful family—even though they had suffered such a horrible loss with the death of his brother, they were so positive, so deeply spiritual and grounded. I loved being at their house—it undid some of the bad things that had happened at my own.

I was going through so many issues with my own dad that I needed to be around someone who was unwaveringly positive. That was Bear—I never heard him say anything negative. He didn't always say a lot. He was a guy of few words, but when he did speak, it was always the truth, delivered kindly and gently.

I remember one day, my dad's girlfriend called me to tell me that my father was in the hospital, that he had cancer. My dad and I weren't speaking, but Bear urged me to go. He told me, "If something happens to your dad, do you really want to go through life being mad at him for being a shitty dad? There's so much more to people. They are who they are. Love is always greater." It would have been so much easier for Bear to pile onto my feelings, to pick up the cross of anger that I was already carrying, but he pushed me to start speaking to my dad again instead. Even when it turned out that my dad did not actually have cancer, but was in the hospital because he had overdosed on meth.

Bear was really big on forgiveness and really big on making it right with people. I guess you could call it taking care of your side of the street, being responsible for your own part in the relationship. In many ways you could call Bear religious, but I think a better word is spiritual. He believed in a lot of what Jesus taught. He went to a Catholic high school, but he was more about the spirit of the Bible than the letter. He just breathed living kindness.

With everything that had happened with my family, my own faith had definitely drifted. Part of my rebellion was rejecting the church, which had been important to my grandparents. But Bear gave me back my spirituality. I believe he brought me back to myself and grounded me at a time when I felt like I was untethered, and most inclined to just float away.

The summer before our senior year was magical. While Bear was not my first everything, he was certainly my first love. And it was a deep one. I had lost my virginity to a guy friend from school down at the beach a few months before I met Bear. I thought it was a good idea at the time because he was nice and respectful, and I trusted him, but it was awkward and terrible all around, and the next day, I regretted it. That regret, compounded by my Catholic guilt, ended up ruining our relationship. In hindsight, I would have much rather had his friendship than his virginity.

Bear and I daydreamed a lot about where we'd go after high school—he thought he'd wear a morning tux to our wedding, that we'd have babies. Bear was an incredible artist, and my primary goal, particularly because I felt so directionless, was to live vicariously through him. When I was in eighth grade, I had asked for a guitar for Christmas, which Santa delivered under the tree. My dad refused to get me lessons, because in his mind, only stoners played guitar. I also used to paint all the time, but my parents assumed that anyone who was artsy also did drugs. I think they felt that by forcing me into soccer, they would be assured that I'd have a future free of partying and hard drugs. What they didn't realize was that by disconnecting me from things I actually cared about, they only made me feel more lost. So at school I threw myself into music, art, drama. And I threw myself into my relationship with Bear, who represented everything I loved and had been denied—everything I hid from my parents at home.

One night, after we had been dating for a few months, I walked Bear from my house to his car. We shared a really passionate kiss—one of those kisses that you feel inside your entire body. As we stood outside in the dry desert heat, he asked me if he could do something. He lifted up my shirt, unhooked my bra and just held me, skin-to-skin. I could feel the reverberations of his heart in my own. It was a quiet moment, not sexual. It was one of the most powerful and moving things I had ever felt with someone.

Bear was such a good artist that the local Starbucks asked to put up a show of his work. He taught himself how to play the piano, how to play the guitar. He was an incredible skateboarder. He was simply perfect, complete and self-assured. Someone who knew what he wanted. He also had opportunities—Berkeley and colleges in New York were into his stuff. I figured my graduation plan could be to just follow him around if he'd let me.

My birthday is in November, and he made me a CD as my gift. His friends mocked him, but I loved it. I've never cared about material things, and if he had gone out and spent money it would have made me uncomfortable. So he made me a mix and told me that every song had meaning to each of us, and to our relationship. He wrote "For Bri" across the jewel case. (My family and friends spell my name Bri.) I still listen to it today, and it brings me back to our entire relationship, to this incredible guy. It's a complete soundtrack to some of the most magical months of my life, of being with someone who made me feel whole. I'm so grateful that he didn't give me a shirt, or something silly that I would have lost or broken over the years. For Christmas, he gave me a Mother Mary necklace—for protection—that I still treasure. I can't remember what I gave him, though I'm sure it was embarrassing. But he gave me a Mother Mary—that was just like him, marking moments like that in ways that were actually meaningful.

On January 18, Bear and I had plans to go and do something. He really wanted to go to the St. Mary's football game, so I told him to come and find me after. Something happened that messed up our plans, and he never came to meet me. It wasn't the age of texting, and so everything was set at the beginning of the night and timed perfectly. If you missed each other, that was your only chance. I was pissed, and we argued. This was really unusual for us, despite my hair-trigger temper. The next day he called me on my house phone. He told me he was going to go skate with his friends and then come find me. We both apologized for the night before and felt silly that it had been enough to make us fight. It was a new day and I couldn't wait to see him later.

That night, January 19, I waited for him at my house alone. My mom went out with her girlfriends, my brother was at a friend's house, and my sister—who had fractured her leg two weeks before and been stuck in bed ever since—had been dragged out of the house and to a movie by her boyfriend.

Bear and his friend Greg were going to pick up our friend Ronnie and then cruise to my house. I knew exactly how long it would take for him to get to me. I remember looking at the clock and thinking, "Dang, I bet he stopped at a party and I'm once again on the back burner." I started to get annoyed, which built into frustration and anger. Then my sister came through the door, wanting to hang out with Bear. She had been walking into the movie theater with her boyfriend when she asked him to drive her home because she felt a strong urge to see us. And then my brother showed up, wanting to see Bear, too. And then my friends Sarah and Val called, wanting to see Bear. Within thirty minutes, I went from sitting and waiting by myself to being surrounded by people who all wanted to see Bear.

I mixed some Ruby Red Squirt with a little vodka from my mom's stash and gave everyone a drink (none for JJ, don't worry). Then I thought, "Oh, Bear's here." I could smell him. I told everyone the boys had finally arrived and walked out to the front. But he wasn't there. I went to the backyard, thinking maybe he had detoured around the house to finish his cigarette. No Bear.

Then the phone rang. It was Bear's older brother, Patrick. He said quietly, "Brie, Bear has been in a really bad accident." Then he went silent, started crying, and hung up on me. My heart dropped, but I didn't think death. Death was impossible. I called him back. "Brie, Bear is dead. He's dead, Brie." I was in the living room and I tried to grab on to the console, but I collapsed onto the floor. Bear was seventeen, he was invincible. I had just spoken to him hours before. I begged God to bring him back, pleading and bargaining with him that it wouldn't be weird if he performed a miracle and restarted his heart—this was Bear. Bear *was* a miracle.

I thought if I could get to the hospital, maybe it would be enough to save him. My girlfriend Val drove me there, running every red light on the way. The only miracle that night was that we didn't die as well. I will always remember how that evening smelled, how I could feel death in the hospital. I sat in the emergency room and waited. When they rolled Greg out, he looked like a marshmallow. I remember thinking that if he was alive, and looked like that, I could only imagine what had happened to Bear.

Greg and Bear were hit by a guy who was racing to a party. He was intoxicated and driving without a license. It was a hit and run, though they caught him and he spent seven years in jail. Bear wasn't wearing a seatbelt and was flung from the car, but they think the rollbar of the truck would have smashed him anyway. Greg thinks they were hit twice, but knows for certain that they hit the gravel in the center of the freeway and rolled. He remembers looking at Bear in the moment after they had been hit, when Greg had lost control of the car. Bear just smiled back at him, like he knew, like he had already transcended his body. When the car stopped rolling, Greg sprinted to Bear and held him in his lap, but Bear was already gone, he had died on impact.

Everyone met up at a house to pray and be together after. I went and, for the first time, felt like I didn't belong. I was the girl from a different high school, and I felt responsible for taking away their best friend. He meant so much to so many different people. One girl muttered under her breath that if he hadn't been on his way to see me, he wouldn't be dead. I wanted to hear that. In retrospect, that is insane, but it was impossible for me to not want to hold some of the responsibility. It gave his death some meaning, and a reason, when it felt like it had neither.

I was in deep crisis and grief, totally ill-equipped to deal with the loss. When you lose a relationship, it can feel like you lose all the memories you shared because they are too painful to remember. And most strangely, you are suddenly left with days full of holes that were once filled up by someone else. Everything has to shift, which is a terrible exercise when you don't want it to. I wanted to hold that space to think about and mourn Bear, not to just absorb the loss and move on. Feeling "normal" again was a terrifying idea. I didn't want a new normal without Bear. Every day, I'd had a routine. I went to school, then to my mom's office, where I had worked as a receptionist since I was fifteen, then to Bear's house until I had to pick up Nicole at the gym where she manned the front desk. Rinse and repeat.

After Bear died, I couldn't go right back to school. I stayed home for several weeks and cried until I was empty. While my friends were busy planning their futures postgraduation, I was just trying to get to the next day. A week ahead seemed impossibly far away. I honestly don't think I would have made it if it weren't for Bear's friends and Bear's mom, who managed somehow to hold us all up in our grief despite her own. I think she knows, I hope she knows, how much that time meant to me. Being a mother now, I can't imagine how she made it through those days, much less how she carried us all through. Bear and his mother shared a strong faith, and just being around her reminded me of him. I could have gone two ways at that time. I could have decided to hate God and tell everyone and everything to fuck itself, but Bear's mom helped me to a different outcome. She helped me to not lose touch with what he had brought into my life—his purpose and his passion. I felt like I had to harness these qualities for myself so they wouldn't be lost. It was far better and more productive than believing he had lived and died for no reason.

I started writing, which felt like a way to communicate directly with him. Actually, it's strange, but the Monday before Bear died we were hanging out at his house. We'd typically start out those nights sitting next to each other on the piano bench, while he serenaded me with songs. His family had a library of VHS cassette tapes—movies like *My Cousin Vinny*, his favorite, and other classics from the eighties and nineties. That night we were watching something we had probably seen a hundred times before, and he turned to me and said something like: "I have this feeling that I'm going to die young, like before I'm thirty." I laughed at what I thought was his fantasy of some rock 'n' roll flameout. I didn't realize at the time that his soul was preparing him for death. It was sending up a little warning flare that some things are too good to stick around for long.

In retrospect, I realize his dog Maggie was acting weird that week, too. She was hovering around him, watching and guarding. I can't help but believe that the gifts he had given me—my Mother Mary necklace, my "For Bri" CD, a clay bear he made for me in pottery class so I'd always have a bear to watch over me at night—were anticipatory totems of protection. They were for when he wouldn't be there himself to protect me.

Earlier that year, the Diamondbacks had won the World Series, and the whole town erupted in celebration. Bear lived by the Heard Museum, devoted to American Indian art. There was a vacant house nearby, and one night we hopped a fence and snuck in, so we could watch the fireworks from inside. It felt like it was our house that night, and we were watching a celebration of our future. Just the two of us, alone in the world, surrounded by colorful bursts of light.

When I'd started dating Bear, I quit soccer. My mom was pissed. Colleges were taking a long look at me, and she thought the possibility of a scholarship was my only chance of going to school. Never mind that I was miserable on the field. "You hate soccer," Bear had said, "so why are you committing yourself to a future where you have to keep playing?" He was right, even though it seemed like a reckless choice at the time, particularly considering I didn't have any other options. "You've got to do what feels right," he always said, "do what makes you happy." It might sound trite, but this was wise counsel from a high school senior. After he was gone, I tried to bury what he wanted for me in my body and use him as my compass.

When I graduated from high school, Bear's mom gave me the portrait that he had painted of me that day in the attic. It was a split face. He had painted a self-portrait to make up the other side and then he hung the pair on his bedroom wall. He told me that at night, the moon would shine across our eyes, lighting us both up. I still have the painting, and I look at it often. I'm lucky that my husband, Bryan, is so unthreatened by my past and is understanding of what Bear continues to mean to me. But then, I often think that Bear sent him my way. Before I left town for California, I went with Bear's family to get bear claw tattoos on my lower abdomen. It's funny, because I dated a lot of guys throughout the years who did not dig them at all. They were freaked out by their presence. I think of them as a gesture of protection from Bear, a way of warding off guys who have no business being in my life. They are a final totem.

I still pray to Bear every day. I ask him for help with difficult situations, I ask him for strength before matches, I ask him for advice about tricky decisions. I ask him if he's doing a big skateboarding ramp up in heaven. If there's a beautiful sunset, I'll ask him if he painted it for me. I have reason to believe that he hears me, because he sends me signs all the time. In particular, he sends me feathers at moments when I need them most. A bit after Bear died, I was in a bookstore with my sister, browsing the self-help aisle (as one does). I was trying to work through my wanderlust and lack of direction. I passed a shelf with a book that was about bears. I picked it up to flip through it and a feather fell to the floor. I walked up to the owner of the bookstore and asked him why a feather, which looked like it had just been plucked off of a bird's ass, was in this book. He looked at me like I was nuts. He took it from me to toss it in the trash, but I asked him if I could keep it. Which made him look at me like I was really nuts. Other times, I've asked Bear if he can hear me, and a song from my "For Bri" CD will come on the radio. To this day it still happens with so much frequency it feels impossible that it's a coincidence. I believe that he is my guardian angel.

A few months after Bear died, I was hanging out at his friend Austin's house. Austin's mom pulled me aside. I thought she just wanted to check in on me, make sure I was eating and sleeping and taking care of myself. But she told me that she had been in the crystal store in town, and a woman who worked there had called out: "There's a young man here." This woman had described what he looked like and said that he was showing her an image of a bear. She said that the young man had been in a car accident and his life was cut short. Austin's mom raised her hand and told the woman she thought she knew who he was, and that he must be trying to reach her. As Austin's mom told me this, I remember looking at her like she was batshit crazy. I wasn't familiar with the concept of psychics and mediums—the Catholic Church, while all about angels, frowns on that sort of thing. Then Austin's mom told me that the woman in the crystal store had mentioned me, as well as Bear's cousin Paul, and that she really needed to speak to us.

I told her I didn't believe in that sort of thing, and she nodded. "I get it, but I wouldn't feel right if I didn't tell you." She handed me the phone number for the medium, whose name was Tricia. I thought about it for a while. I believed in angels and thought I had seen Bear a number of times. I dreamed about him constantly. So I went to the store, which was called A Peace of the Universe, and found Tricia, to test her. "Listen," I said, "I don't know anything about this stuff, and I'm not going to sit here and tell you about my life. What is it exactly that you need?" I was just a high school kid, and I'm sure she didn't really know what to do with me either. But she sat me down and began to channel Bear. I said nothing.

She told me things, intimate things, that only the two of us knew. She brought up the night we spent in the vacant house watching the fireworks, which was something Bear and I had kept as a secret for ourselves. I immediately started to bawl and asked her how the fuck she could possibly know any of it. (I definitely said "fuck"; I was upset.) "Brie, he's telling me." That first reading was one of the craziest experiences of my life, and that's saying a lot from a WWE wrestler. She asked me if I had been at the cemetery that morning putting flowers on his grave. She went on: "He said you were crying really, really hard—that you blame yourself." I told her that it was true, I had been there that morning and I did feel responsible. She replied, "There was a reason for his death—I know it seems impossible, but there was a reason. You have to stop blaming yourself."

Then, she just let Bear speak. It was her voice, but it was his lingo. It was what he would say and how he would say it. When he was done, Tricia said: "He's rubbing your earlobes right now. Is that a thing?" I gasped. Bear used to rub my earlobes all the time, whenever we were watching a movie, or driving, or he just felt like reaching over and touching me. When his casket was going into the ground, his mom had reached over to rub my earlobes in his stead, because I was so upset.

Tricia ended up becoming a really important part of my life until I moved to San Diego. She was a different type of grief counselor, but one that I desperately needed. While these moments of reconnection and conversation with Bear didn't take away the pain of losing him, they helped me tremendously because I could feel him. I could hear the proof that he was still there, that he could hear me, that we were still deeply connected.

I lost touch with Tricia over the years, though other mediums and healers have come in and out of my life as I've needed them. Judy, who owned the shop, was another pillar of strength, doling out a hug to anybody who needed one. All of my girlfriends started going there, just for hugs from Judy. Like me, they all came from families of divorce, families with shitty dads. She had the power to make you feel like the world was actually a really wonderful place, that all would be well. I was back in Scottsdale a couple of years ago and went by to see her after nearly a decade. As fate would have it, it was her last week in the store. She felt she was being called to move to the East Coast to open a store, that the people there needed her more. I had given her something of Bear's to put on the wall, and it was still there.

When you're a kid, you think you'll live forever. Even adulthood, with kids and responsibilities, feels like it is decades away.

When I lost Bear, I began to look at life differently. The day he died, he had skateboarded, gone to Jack in the Box with his friends, barbecued with his family. All in all, a beautiful and simple day that ended badly. I know that every day is a new day, and that I'm lucky to wake up and have it. I shouldn't take those small pleasures, like greasy fast-food fries or a really fun night out with friends, for granted. I know that my only real concern should be living how it feels right and honest to live. It is never worth wasting energy on those who might judge or disagree with the choices that I've made. When I emerged from constant tears and heartbreak, I felt like a liberated spiritual being, free to love and live every moment. It is how you live when you feel like you've lost one of the things that is most valuable, when you realize that death might not necessarily be the end, and when you accept that we might just have a far greater purpose here.

I'd shed all my tears for Bear. Nothing else could make me cry—not my abysmal 2.7 GPA, not the way I'd lost my virginity, not anything going on at home or with soccer. Nothing sucks more than dying. I could do really badly on my SATs—which I did!—but death is worse. Sure, my life wasn't perfect, but things could be so, so much worse.

When I graduated, I had to get out of Phoenix because everything reminded me of Bear. I needed a fresh start, where I wouldn't be triggered by . . . everywhere. My house, his house, the hole-in-the-wall Mexican joint off Camelback Road where he took me for burritos on one of our first official dates. He even drew something on the napkin for the waiter. If you've lost someone in a tragic way, when you are wholly unprepared for their passing, then you know that there is no forgetting. I'm sure that is true for those who've had long goodbyes and peaceful ends, too. People are always scared to mention someone you've lost. I think they're afraid that maybe you've forgotten that that person is gone, and they're reminding you of something painful. But that's not how it actually is—the people you lose live in your mind, your heart, your very being, in a way that is constant. Talking about them feels good—even if it might also bring tears—because it's a way of bringing them to life again, of indulging in memories. There is no getting over it. There is only learning to live with it.

The affirmation from Tricia also helped me learn how to trust my own gut, and tap into my intuition. I know, when I feel a certain internal pressure, or shove, that I should pay attention. It feels like Bear pushing me forward. In fact, I think it was Bear, knowing how much I love music, and art, and drama, who pushed me toward Los Angeles and WWE. Like most people, I was really only comfortable when I was good at something, when success was pretty certain. Blind leaps of faith were really fucking scary. When you have a lot of money, you can make mistakes and fall back into a safety net. I didn't have any dough for missteps, but the push was persistent. If someone had told me my senior year that I was going to become a WWE wrestler, I would have told them, "No way." But I think Bear knew it was the right thing for me—it was Broadway, it was art, it was sport. When we were kids, guys used to call Nicole and me the Basham Sisters, after the pro wrestlers Doug and Danny Basham. It was our personalities, our aggressiveness, the fact that Nicole and I both really liked to brawl. If Bear could have been in the stands watching us, he would have loved it, this funny totally unlikely future in WWE. He would have loved it because *I* love it. After all, the only thing he really wanted for me was to stand up and fight for what I want.

Who knows if my relationship with Bear would have even survived high school; who knows where our lives would have gone. It is a weird thing, to have a relationship that was never allowed to complete itself, at such a young age, when you are keyed up to love with such abandon. When it feels so magical. There was no closure, no sabotage, no fighting until we hated each other. As we get older and wiser and a bit more seasoned, we make choices in relationships that transcend that beginning honeymoon phase— everything is more measured, more sustainable. I'm so grateful that Bryan is the man he is. He can hold all of me, even the parts that will always be a little broken. I'm free to be sad when I'm sad, without judgment or feeling like I need to hide in the bathroom to cry. My residual grief is not an affront to him or diminishing of all the wonderful people and things that I now have in my life. He understands that my heart is fully his—but that there's room in there to celebrate and remember Bear, too. I like to think that Bear helped make me who I am. By loving me, Bryan's love extends to Bear as well.

# CHAPTER 4

# MY OTHER BIG BREAK

## 1993-2007
### Phoenix, Arizona

## Nicole

I kicked the soccer ball for the first time when I was in fifth grade. And when I say I kicked it, I mean I whaled on it. It had been my parents' idea to put me in club soccer—I was extremely athletic and very aggressive, which roughly translated to a "sports for her" decision. Though for my parents, athletics translated to free college and the promise that I would be too busy to become a drug addict or have an active dating life, so there was that, too. In contrast, they put Brie in ballet. That was short-lived, as they made her start playing soccer a year later, I think in part because I was so good at it. It seemed inevitable that she would be, too. While Brie is also very athletic, she took soccer for what it was and ultimately quit in high school. It didn't really speak to her. I, on the other hand, wanted to "go HAM." I took that shit seriously. I played sweeper, which meant that beyond being a starter (the ultimate honor), I typically stayed on the field for the entire game. This was rare in fifth grade, when there was pressure to give all kids equal playing time and show no signs of favoritism. But I was a closer. I was good.

Soccer was a big deal in Arizona, and our coaches were former professional players from Europe. It was a no-bullshit, we're-not-just-here-to-tool-around-and-kill-the-afternoon approach to the game. Even in fifth grade, we were on that field to win—and I loved it. I wanted to be depended on in that way. I relished the faith and trust the coaches and other players put on me. We traveled as far as Washington, D.C., for tournaments, which meant that soccer could literally take me far away from home. The promise of a life that wasn't tethered to Arizona was very appealing at the time. It seemed like a real ticket out.

I threw myself into soccer with so much abandon, because not only was I good at it (and what kid doesn't love that type of affirmation?) and very, very competitive, but also because it provided me with the structure, schedule, and boundaries that my parents weren't able to construct at home. My coaches were strict—mandatory curfews, bedtimes, specific pregame meal plans. I needed that sort of oversight from adults who were invested in my future, who cared about my well-being, who treasured me and thought I was really worth something. My parents needed it, too, because it created a way for them to really show up for me. My parents rarely missed games. My mom would run up and down the sidelines cheering us on. My parents loved us, but the scene at home was volatile, at best. Soccer was anything but—as dependable and orderly as possible, controlled for all variables and factors.

I was also very good at track. When I made it to regionals in fifth grade, I was the youngest competitive runner to break the track records in the 400 and the 800 in Arizona. I was super fast. I made it to regionals one year, which were held at UCLA. It was the first time I was away from Brie—I was there for a week, and so we would write each other letters. I think this was the first time that our paths ever diverged, that something separated us and put physical distance between us. I bombed my race. The girl who I really looked up to slipped and fell in the race before mine. It really shook me and I couldn't get my head into my run. I pretty much jogged. It was the first time I had ever experienced being taken out of the game—I couldn't get back into it.

Throughout high school, I spent my summers doing Olympic development programs. At that time, women did okay in the pro league—it seemed like a decent living if you could line up some endorsements. That was really the only path to the World Cup, which was, of course, the ultimate dream. But my first priority with kicking that ball was to use it to get my college education paid for. I wasn't a major student. As my sister and I say, we never learned how to talk good. But I knew I needed some sort of degree if I wanted to have a future. It all seemed within reach, too, because when I was in high school I would get pulled up into

Arizona State University scrimmages. My ultimate plan was to have soccer take me away from home.

It's funny, because those scrimmages were some of the first times that I encountered eye rolls as an upstart. I would head onto the field, and to be fair, I was cocky as shit. The older girls would just send hate rays my way. I didn't care at all. In fact, it just made me more driven, more competitive, more inclined to take the ball away from them. I didn't know it at the time, but it was a good training ground for WWE locker rooms. For moving through negative energy and that unbridled hope for my failure. On that field, I learned how to thrive in the toxic stew, to use it to my advantage.

And I was aggressive, undeniably. I once got a red card (not my only one), because this girl took out Brie by yanking her down backwards by her shirt. If anyone was going to do that to her, it was going to be me! I screamed, "Don't touch my sister!" and slammed that girl into the ground repeatedly. Obviously, a total overreaction, but people learned not to fuck with my sister! I got into a lot of fights and would yell at the coaches. I was a hothead, and I felt like I had nothing to lose. During one game we were playing in Arcadia, the crowd in the stands started yelling, "Beaners! Beaners! Go back to Mexico!" So I slide-tackled their star girl, looked at the crowd, and threw my hands up into the victory sign. They used to call me "The Rock."

I've always maintained that in order to do well at sports, you have to have a certain amount of confidence—maybe cockiness— but fearlessness for sure. Since fifth grade, I'd always made All

State, or been MVP. My senior year I really wanted to be Player of the Year, which was a senior-year-only award. The rumor was that it was mine, even though a lot of the other coaches and players hated me (as mentioned, I had a mouth on me). Then a week before State, a week before that award might have been mine, a forward on the other team had a breakaway, and I did a slide tackle—and she kicked me in the shin and broke my tibia in half.

Out on that field that day, I couldn't move—my left side was in complete shock. My dad had to carry me to the sidelines. The firefighters came, though I assured them that nothing was broken. They played along with the charade, even though they knew just from looking at my leg that I was in serious trouble. My parents couldn't afford an ambulance, and so the firefighters carried me to my dad's pickup truck, and he drove me to the hospital, where I sat in the waiting room for hours. By the time they brought me back, my leg was too swollen for surgery—the doctor wanted to operate but felt like it was too risky because of the swelling and potential for blood clots. They put me in a cast and sent me home for two weeks to wait until my leg deflated. To get the cast on right—from hip to heel—they had to straighten my leg and flex my foot. Despite my incredibly high pain tolerance, I screamed bloody murder. I haven't experienced childbirth, but to this day, it was one of the most painful experiences of my life. And I've been flung from the ring into tables.

When my parents divorced a few years prior, our insurance had changed—and not for the better. When I was fourteen, I had double knee surgery because there was no cartilage between my knee joint and my leg (patellofemoral syndrome), and I was able to have it done under the supervision of a really good surgeon. But this time, it was different. The first attempt to put a rod and three screws into my leg did not work—so they had to redo the surgery three weeks later. All of my college offers were rescinded since it wasn't clear that I would ever be able to walk properly again, much less play competitive soccer. I can't really blame those coaches: I was stuck in bed. When I was up on my feet, I had to walk with a cane—my future as an athlete certainly wasn't assured. And then two weeks after I broke my leg, Bear died.

The night that Bear died, my high school boyfriend, who we'll call Ken, had finally convinced me to get out of the house. I had been bedridden for two weeks, and getting up required a massive amount of energy— plus, my entire future had collapsed and I was pretty depressed. Ken was a football player and drove a green Camaro (of course), which was extra impossible to maneuver my leg into. We made it to the movie theater, and I was limping in on crutches, when I felt a strong urge to go home to be with Brie and Bear. Ken was annoyed—it had taken a lot of effort to get me there. But I made him take me back. He understood what was happening at home, as he had come from a broken family, too. Thank God I felt the pull to leave. Thank God I hadn't been in a movie when she got that call.

After Bear died, our home was a terrible scene. We had moved into a smaller house when my parents divorced, and Brie and I were sharing a room. At night, she cried inconsolably—her body just heaving in pain. I felt so far away from her, like I couldn't possibly reach her in her grief. I also couldn't lay any of my own sadness on her either. It didn't help that I was immobile. At night, I would army crawl and drag myself across the floor to get into bed with her and try to calm her down. We were just two girls in Arizona with collapsed dreams and uncertain futures. Brie, in particular, felt like everything she loved had been taken away.

After Bear died, I had an appointment for my screws to come out. My mom was out of town, so she asked my dad to take me. He was really not in a good place—and we really weren't speaking. After, I was recovering at his house. He and Ken started fighting about something stupid, I think it was about who was getting more attention from me. They got into a yelling fight, and then both took off. My dad to walk down the freeway, Ken in his green Camaro. They both just ditched me, with nobody to even help me go to the bathroom. I think my dad was on mushrooms that day—though it was never easy to tell when he was using and when he was not—but drugs certainly fueled his rage. It was a weird time, the end-cap to a pretty terrible four-year run. It only underlined for me and Brie that we needed to get the hell out of Arizona. We needed a fresh start far away.

My grandparents had a little bit to give for college, but my parents weren't in any situation to pay for undergrad for two of us. I had always loved interior design and went to ASU to check out their program. I ultimately didn't feel like I could take out student loans and ever be certain I could pay them back. I just couldn't afford college, but I wanted out of Arizona—it was just too full of bad memories.

I thought about going to cosmetology school, since I was good at doing hair. I went to beauty school orientation, but it didn't appeal. As graduation approached, Brie and I decided to pack our bags and head to San Diego, to Grossmont Community College. Anything seemed better than home. Brie and I knew we could hustle for cash—we had both worked since we were fifteen. We'd been hostesses at Seafood Central, and I'd worked as a receptionist for my mom and at a local gym, the Village. We figured if we were responsible for ourselves, without the drama of home holding us back, it could only get better.

We did a year at Grossmont and then went to Los Angeles. Then I ended up back in San Diego with my boyfriend, the professional snowboarder. I felt like I needed to make something of myself. Even though I was old for community college, twenty-one or twenty-two, I showed up at the soccer field. Fortunately, the coach knew who I was from my high school career, and he insisted that I walk on. I demurred, but he told me to run a mile, right there. I was woefully out of shape, but he yelled "Go, go, go" the entire time. I booked it until I almost passed out. He told me to make it to my classes, keep my grades up, and I joined the team. At that point, I felt a little awkward about my age—the other girls were always hitting me up to buy them beer. When the driver of one of the vans failed to show up for a tournament, I was the only player old enough to take the wheel of a rental car and drive instead. I played there for a year and took them to a State Championship, earning MVP. This was despite the fact that I got a stress fracture in my right foot and had to learn how to kick with my left. The girls begged me to stay for another season. The coach thought I had a viable shot of making it as a professional player in Italy, but I was still with my professional snowboarding boyfriend. I knew that would be a total disaster if I moved to Europe. And by that point, Brie called me about the WWE audition—I watched the girls on *Raw* and then drove up to L.A. to try out.

Looking back on my senior year in high school, it's hard not to be angry. I pushed myself so hard to funnel all of my energy into soccer, and my education, social life, and SATs all suffered a lot for it. Then I ended up with a shitty-ass surgeon and the minimum requirement of physical therapy. We didn't have good insurance, which definitely didn't help. But my parents and I didn't advocate for me at all either. We didn't push enough on my behalf, demand better care, or research my surgeon before letting him fuck up my leg. Being a professional athlete now, with resources, I realize how much more could have been done for me. How important it is to ask questions, research, explore all channels, and ask for help. I believe the outcome could have been so much better. Maybe that college scholarship could have been resurrected.

I will say that my coach, Matt Potter, who had been with us since we started playing in fifth grade, did try to help. He knew how rough it was at home, and he treated us at times like we were his own kids. He would come and meet me outside of practice and get me training and moving again—kicking the ball, getting some mobility back. Throughout my life—and like Blanche DuBois—I've come to depend on the kindness of strangers.

I was still young, with my whole life in front of me. But it's a strange experience when your best laid plans, everything you've ever counted on, disintegrate. And it's a stranger feeling when that future was contingent on your body, which you've always had complete control over. That period in my life was dark for many reasons, but it was really the first time that I felt like I personally hit a wall. I had lost the thing that most defined me. In retrospect, as angry as it made me, I wouldn't have had my life turn out any differently. Italy would have been fun and all, but women's wrestling, and standing behind this movement of female empowerment in the ring—the creation of real-life sheros—has inarguably been a much more incredible adventure to join and lead.

And it feels like the fact that Brie and I were both rerouted on this path was anything but luck. After Bear died, Brie became very spiritual. Fortunately, a fair amount of that rubbed off on me. It came from watching her prevail over dark, dark grief, but also from her faith that there is something on the other side. That life has a much greater purpose than it might sometimes seem to have on the surface. I'm not saying that there was divine intervention in my leg break, but I do think that this bigger context—maybe we're not just here to live and die—helped me turn that course correction into something positive. I've always found that I'm most successful when I mix a certain amount of everything-happens-for-a-reason fatalism with driving really hard for what I want. It helps me manage my expectations for the moments when I don't get what I want, while also keeping me feeling like I am in the driver's seat and capable of, and responsible for, directing my life.

So I wish I could say that I immediately went and capitalized on and maximized this post-soccer freedom, but not so fast. First, I had to marry and then divorce my high school boyfriend, Ken. Before I get into what he meant to me, and why we eloped to a Las Vegas chapel, I need to back up to the darker undercurrent of high school. There were some experiences I wish I could forget, but I feel, more than ever at this point in the culture, like I need to revisit and share.

My dad was controlling, abusive, and strict, and he had never really let me speak to boys. So when my parents finally divorced when I was fifteen, I lost my virginity—on the floor of a Hyatt hotel room on the 4th of July. "Lost my virginity" is very inaccurate, actually. My virginity was stolen from me, without my consent. I was raped, by a guy I thought was a friend, while I was passed out at a party. I'd had too many beers, and maybe some shots of hard alcohol, and I only woke up because my stomach hurt—I came to, and this guy was both on top of me and inside of me. I pushed him off and ran out of the room—he followed me down the hall and asked me if this meant we were now boyfriend/girlfriend.

It is fucked up—shocking in retrospect—that it never occurred to me to call the police. I didn't even tell my sister because by admitting that it had happened, it became true, it became fact. He didn't apologize, he didn't worry about getting in trouble. He thought that by taking advantage of me, he should now have official and full access to me. That this attack would actually make me his, in a celebrated social way. I get enraged even writing about this now. I know I was not the only girl in our high school who was violated like that and then expected to shrug it off the next day—this is what it was like. There was no education around it, no awareness, no five-point plan should it happen to you. And man do I pray things are different now, that girls realize that if something that horrendous and sickening happens to them, they can and should say and do something. I wish I had known that I could have taken away his future the way he had taken something so sacred away from me. Something I was waiting to share with someone I loved, at the time of my choice. While I didn't know what to do about it, I had even less of a clue how to address the shame and revolting feelings of ickiness that permeated my whole being. I had never even seen a penis, yet I was no longer a virgin.

I actually had a boyfriend at the time—an older guy who went to another high school in town. He had been totally respectful of me, and we had never done anything beyond kissing. I didn't tell him that I had been raped, but I did tell him I was ready to have sex. I wanted so desperately to erase what had happened and replace it with a new first, positive experience that felt special. He was surprised—when you're in high school, you typically follow the bases very slowly. I don't remember if he'd had sex before, but when we started, and he said, "You're not a virgin," I protested, but I was crushed (side note: What a dick!). The sex we had felt dirty and horrible.

A few months later, I went to a modeling competition with a friend in California. We met two guys who invited us back to their hotel room. My friend was really excited about the invitation and begged me to go, even though they gave me the creeps. I tried to convince her that it was a bad idea. We were sixteen, they were college age, if not in their mid-twenties, and it felt dangerous and wrong. But I finally relented. We sat on the edge of the bed while they tried to get us to drink from a jug of orange juice and vodka. I refused and refused again and again, until I finally relented. I thought that if I gave in on this, maybe they'd leave me alone. I hadn't drunk very much before I felt really dizzy and stood up to go to the bathroom, thinking I might vomit. One of the guys followed me in and bashed my head against the bathroom sink—I came to when he accidentally switched on the blow-dryer with his elbow. I had clearly been roofied—I was groggy, and I couldn't see straight, but I could see four condom wrappers littered across the bathroom floor and realized that I had been raped. I hit him in the face and ran from the bathroom—my friend was gone and the door was open. I took off into the night, sprinting across empty fields until I made it back to the hotel where we were staying with her mom.

My friend was there. She had left me behind and run. But she had also been raped and was hysterical and in the shower. Her mom held me until I calmed down. Then, for some reason, the three of us decided not to call the police, not to tell anyone. We all decided to pretend like it had never happened. Even my mom is learning about this for the first time in this book. We certainly didn't do the right thing by failing to call the cops. But in a fucked-up way, I think we all felt responsible. Her mom, for failing to protect us. The two of us, for willingly going to the guys' rooms, for drinking alcohol illegally.

The #MeToo movement both enthralls me with its potential and reminds me why rape and sexual assault are a double slap for women. There is the horrible offense in the moment, and then the shame and blame that follow and feel almost worse than the original pain. When something like this happens to you, you understand the blame-the-victim mentality, how easy it is to feel shame rather than anger, how easy it is to feel like you could have stopped it yourself. The "if onlys," the "why didn't I's . . ."

I count myself lucky because I was unconscious for both rapes. But the other details, like the faces of all three men, the condom wrappers, the sound of the blow-dryer—it's all seared into my mind. If I had been aware of what was happening to me in the moment, I would never have been able to escape it, or get over it. I can imagine how the consciousness—and the feelings of helplessness to stop the assaults—could have really ruined my life.

After these two incidents, I fell into a deep depression. When my mom was at work, I would go into her closet and shut the door and cry. I would just sit there, among a sea of her very work-appropriate Nine West heels. I gained visible weight, probably the first time that I became the "bigger" sister of the two of us. It was a physical manifestation of holding on to all these secrets as a sixteen-year-old. I was eating my feelings in an attempt to push the depression down, to somehow digest it. I didn't want anyone to know what had happened. I didn't even tell Brie until many years later. I had no tools for processing the trauma except to try to bury it deep within and pretend like neither episode had ever happened. I was just not equipped.

Later that summer, I met the guy who would become my high school love. He held this promise of safety, of starting over. Ken and I first talked at a party. I was hanging out in a hot tub, waiting for this hot senior I had a crush on to come back. Ken climbed in to keep me company, and then we really connected. I remember thinking that the water made his blue eyes sparkle. He was so handsome, and he had a lot of muscles for a high school kid; he seemed safe and protective. I totally forgot about the hot senior. Nothing happened that night with Ken, which made him seem even safer. He was not a guy who would rape a passed-out girl in a hotel room. After that night we started talking on the phone, and on AOL Messenger. My screen name was PNKDMND, which I picked because I thought "pink diamond" evoked Marilyn Monroe. I didn't know that it was a euphemism for a vagina. And it kind of fits me, don't you think?

A few weeks later, Ken and I hooked up for the first time, at a high school party. I was wearing platform Vans with a four-inch lift, and I never took them off even though I pretty much ditched the rest of my clothing. I was like a dude who wears his socks in bed (I must have been really into those Vans). We were hooking up in an empty bedroom, and then everyone at the party rushed in to bust us. From that point on we were inseparable.

We would hang out at school, after school, at night—he pretty much lived with us by our senior year. He also came from a broken home, and we remade our families in each other. I wanted to be his everything, and he wanted to be my everything, too. We were bunny rabbits—rabid bunnies, actually—looking for anywhere and everywhere to have sex. The middle school baseball diamond, the football field, his Camaro.

Ken was a hothead and was extremely protective. (He even tried to fight a lecherous teacher, who he thought looked at me inappropriately.) I thrived on his desire to stick up for me at every opportunity. I so desperately wanted a guy to make me feel safe, to undo all the bad things that had happened to me. Ken made it feel like love means violent protection—like the world is unsafe without a knight charging with a drawn sword. It squared with my childhood. It squared with what happened to me in my teens. He looked for fights. One time he got jumped by a group of kids. They came into the locker room after a game, when he was alone, and hit him across the back of the head with a bat before punching in his skull with brass knuckles. To this day, I don't know why they had him in their sights. But they had even created a website in advance to commemorate the day that Ken would die—then they set out to fulfill their mission. They were all expelled.

That wasn't his only rodeo in the hospital either. Another time—I think it was for a blood clot—he had to spend a few nights there. When his parents would leave, we'd have sex in his hospital bed—just two kids thinking they were adults. We loved to see how sex would make his heart rate go up, because he was attached to all the machines. I want to die now thinking about it. Obviously the nurses probably had to watch this entire, hilarious spectacle from their station down the hall, while rolling their eyes. Although we'd both had sex before, our relationship was the first time that either of us had really experienced someone's body. I know I've always been a sexual person—I have the middle school journals to prove that—but I think I was partly so attached to Ken because I felt like I could find good touch with him. Enough good touch to take all those bad touches away.

We were kind of lost and were each other's first love—defining what that meant as we went along. We fell hard. It was that first high-school-sweetheart love that's a dumpster fire of lust. In many ways we were completely out of control. The sex, yes, but also the addiction to high drama. We thought that's what it was supposed to feel like. We often had terrible, even violent fights. We both knew that it wasn't healthy or sustainable. But we also couldn't quit the drama or each other. We were like addicts.

## Brie

Ken was a good guy, but the two of them together was not a good combination. He was jealous and controlling, and that was hard for me to see. They would fight all the time, including physically.

I remember one time, Bear and I were hanging out at our house and Nicole and Ken were there. I don't know how it escalated, but they started arguing in front of us. Then suddenly they started wrestling, just throwing each other around my mom's living room. Bear intervened and tried to stop it—he was trying to push them apart when Nicole reached over and just ripped Ken's shirt off his body. Then Ken took off in his green Camaro. I remember thinking, "Can't we all just be normal for one single day?"

## Nicole

A week after graduation, Brie and I moved to California. We were so desperate to get away, to leave all of our bad memories in Arizona behind. The place was tainted, dark. It was a place from which we needed to escape. Ken decided to move to San Diego, too. That's the point when our relationship really fell off a cliff. It was a messed-up situation, because I wanted freedom and complete liberation from the past. Ken reminded me of everything that had happened that was bad. But he had also been my lifeboat for most of it. He would continue to be the person I clung to when things got bad, and I kind of resented him for it. Rinse and repeat.

The fact that I didn't want to look back and didn't want to be tethered to the memories won out in the end. I just wanted to forget. So I treated Ken really poorly. We began a cycle of two weeks on, two weeks off that pretty much went like this: I would clamor for my freedom, and then something would happen that would make me feel bad, or unsafe, or in need of protection, and I would call him. When I felt safe once more, I would dump him again. We had gone through so much shit together, we could never fully let each other go. It makes me feel terrible to recount this, because he didn't deserve any of it.

Ultimately, he went to boot camp because he also wanted to change his life. And I wanted to move to Los Angeles. I missed him a lot while he was away, and I made that very known to him. Then someone planted it in our heads that if we were married he wouldn't be sent abroad to serve, and so we drove to Vegas and got hitched. Internet research at the time was not my friend. I was in a sweatshirt, Uggs, my hair up in a messy bun—it was very Britney Spears. As I walked down the aisle, I thought, "What the hell am I doing and how do I get out of this?"

We never lived together. I never took his last name. He ended up being shipped off to war despite our marriage certificate. That happened when we weren't actually together as a couple anymore and were dating other people, which I think I used as justification for asking him for a divorce when he was away. I shouldn't have done that. I should have waited until he came home to ask him to let me go. I definitely owed him that, even though I ultimately knew that our attachment wasn't healthy and our relationship wasn't good for either of us anymore.

By the end I hated the person I was with him. He made me crazy, evil almost, in a way that felt like I was possessed, like I wasn't myself. When you're young, I don't think you realize that there are other ways to end a relationship besides killing it. Instead, we went down a different path, a destructive, let'sdestroy-ourselves-as-we-destroy-this-romance journey that ultimately created so much more pain. It was on-again, off-again throughout, and I was typically the person driving the status. Every time I felt needy, I got him back; then I would break up with him again. It was not kind. I was in complete sabotage mode, I think probably because, deep down, I thought it would be easier to drive him away than to choose to really leave and fully shut the door. I didn't know if I could hold that responsibility of ending the relationship, and I knew we would keep coming back together, even though it was clearly not the right thing, unless we did so much damage that we burned the house completely down. It's not until you're older that you realize that there are much kinder ways to let things resolve. But as I said, drama was our primary means of communication—and it always felt high-stakes, high-emotion.

I saw him years later, at the funeral of a mutual friend. It was a devastating loss—one of those people who was beloved by many—the life of the party, the class clown, the person you can't imagine not being there anymore. He and Ken were like brothers, truly, in that they knew each other's secrets and had been there through tough times. But it was clear that Ken did not want to speak to me, and so I gave him space. There are very few people I have loved in my life, and Ken was one of them. I will always send him love. I always keep him in my prayers.

I have daddy issues. I'm needy. I have to know someone is there who I can talk to and lean on. As much as I crave freedom—romantic and otherwise—I struggle to stay single. Fortunately,

I don't feel like I remake all of the same mistakes from guy to guy. In retrospect, every one of them seems like it was a course correction on the last. I really believe that early, formative relationships do the lion's share of the work of showing you what you can and cannot tolerate in love and what you ultimately value in a partner. I also believe that when you're young, one of the lines you have to watch is that of codependency. In the process of giving yourself wholly over to a relationship, you have to learn how to find where you end and someone else begins. While Ken was more dependent on me by the end, I got to really sample the other side of the equation next. Enter Jake.

I met Jake when Brie and I had been hired to dress up as naughty nurses for a magazine shoot with him. He was really, really late. Rudely, horribly late. When he finally decided to grace us with his presence, he walked in, looked at me, and said, "My dream girl." My reaction? "Eww . . . what?" I was nineteen and he was twenty-nine. I told him we'd only hang out with him if he went and bought us beer. He was a big-deal Mexican pro athlete, who used to wear these sports jerseys. He was exactly my type. Tough, gangster-ish, built. He was also exceptionally charming and funny and really sweet. I thought he was definitely going to be the love of my life. While he had many wonderful qualities, Jake was also jealous and possessive. We both were in our own ways. I was still at that point in life where I thought love should be dramatic and all-consuming. To be fair, I hadn't seen a real model of something more sustainable growing up. I assumed it was perfectly normal to both hate and love someone within the span of twenty minutes—to fight aggressively and then want to make up and have sex minutes later.

The fact that Jake was ten years older than me makes a lot of sense when I look back. To this day I struggle with my desperate desire for a father figure—someone to tell me what to do, put a fence around me in some ways, be my protector. He did and was all of those things. I completely put my own life on the back burner. This was convenient in many ways because I didn't really know what I wanted my life to be, and his life was pretty great. So I followed him around for two-and-a-half-years—to Alaska, to the X Games, to wherever he determined we should go next. I really just checked out, which flipped Brie out. Rightly, she pointed out to me that I was living for Jake. I had stopped doing things with my friends, and I had given up on my own life goals. I think that it's moments like these that can fully derail women. It's hard to get it going in your early twenties, as every step feels momentous. You have no traction or experience under your belt, and you don't have a network of people who can guide you or help you to your next big break. I've watched friends, even with fancy degrees from four-year colleges, just kind of blow it. They didn't push aggressively against those moments of not knowing WTF to do with their lives. It seems that if you leave it to life to figure it out for you, it won't always turn out for the best.

I remember going to a Blockbuster (RIP) with Jake to rent a movie. We walked past the WWE pay-per-view section. Not surprisingly, he was furious about my WWE contract. In fact, I'm kind of surprised I actually carried through with the audition knowing he would not be supportive. He was mad because it would take me to Tampa, instead of to Salt Lake City, where he primarily lived. Plus he was really uncomfortable with the prospect of the guys. Honestly, that was the last thing on my mind. When it's your job, you're not really checking out the dudes in their tights and trunks (though admittedly, there were a lot of backstage shenanigans at that point in WWE history). He came to visit me once, saw the dudes, and just lost it. I think Jake's jealousy was probably more of a function of his own struggles with fidelity. He often told me that if we stayed together, he'd probably cheat on me. It was a messed-up thing to say, but I appreciated his honesty. Also, I've learned along the way that if someone is jealous in a way that doesn't seem deserved at all, it's probably because they themselves shouldn't be trusted.

We had been together for two-and-a-half-years, and I thought we would be together forever. But our relationship unraveled in a few short months. I knew I'd found my true calling in the wrestling ring in Florida, but it was still really hard on me to let that relationship go. I was so wrapped up in him, and wanted to please him so desperately, that I was crushed when he broke up with me. We had a deep connection, particularly in the bedroom. We had been inseparable until wrestling came between us. The jealousy was exhausting and unsustainable, but it still didn't feel like ending it was my choice.

Obviously, the end of our relationship was the right thing. It was definitely the right thing for my time at FCW, where Brie and I were training in developmental. Wrestling is consuming. It's a strange, insular world, and it's best pursued when you can keep your head fully in the ring without distractions from loved ones who are far away. So even though I was depressed—devastated, really—that Jake had broken up with me, it was way better for my career. I could be fully physically present. It also established wrestling as the other lover—the thing I wanted more than the love of my life. With everything that I had sacrificed, there was no way I was backing down from making it to the main roster. Even if I had to fight a lot of girls to get there.

In making it as a professional athlete, I was also able to re-connect with the primary positive identity of my childhood. I took ahold of that athlete plot line again. And going back to that, re-claiming that title, allowed me to vanquish some of the darker memories from Arizona, too. I acknowledged that I could be the athletic star I remembered without carrying my victimhood into the future. I was a warrior. I was a superhero. And most impor-tant, I had learned how to use my body to fight back.

# CHAPTER 5

# HEEL, YES!

## 2007–2012

Tampa, Florida

San Diego, California

*Brie*

Our very first live wrestling match took place in a Jewish Community Center in Tampa. Nicole and I were playing up the sexy tomboy jock gimmick. We went to the high school sporting goods supply store for gear and bought Tampa Bay Buccaneers jerseys and lace-up football pants, which we extended into bell bottoms with help from a local seamstress. We stood around in the arts and crafts room at the center and waited until it was our turn. When you're on the WWE main roster, they count you down until you hear your entrance music kick in. But when you're wrestling at the local JCC, you hide behind a curtain, or in the arts and crafts room, and you can't hear jack shit. We kept peeking out thinking that they were playing our music. I wanted to vomit, cry, quit.

There were probably only eighty people in the crowd, max, including our mom, but the stakes still felt high. Nicole and I were wrestling Krissy Vaine and Nattie Neidhart, who were nice enough to put us over—i.e., to let us win. Now, it's never your call whether you get to win or lose, but you can make your opponent's victory unpleasant if you want, and a lot of women choose that path. Nattie and Krissy were never like that, though. They were happy for us to get a win right out of the gate. It was nice of them to do it without putting up a fuss—both of them were big factors in our early growth as wrestlers because they were some of the only supportive faces in the locker room. Nattie, in particular, taught us the ropes, the ring, the rules.

It was our first match, so of course it left an indelible mark. What was also incredible about that day was that we met fans there who have followed us to this day—they still meet us at the Tampa airport when we fly into town for WWE. After that first match, they came up to us at the JCC snack bar and asked for our autographs, and it felt amazing. If you're curious about what making it as a wrestler is really like, *The Wrestler*, starring Mickey Rourke, is a heartbreaking must-watch. It's pretty accurate: church parking lots, rec centers . . . really anywhere that has room for a ring and a few stands. You're doing signings at picnic tables, sitting around for thirty minutes or so just waiting for a handful of people to come for an autograph. There are many moments when you feel like a fool. But you have to start somewhere, and we were grateful to be there.

## Nicole

The gnarliest early match was at the flea market. They put up a tarp next to a stall selling dream catchers, and we were expected to change in there, more or less out on display for the strolling shoppers who were looking for bargains, not half-naked wrestlers. The ring itself was in the parking lot. It was scorching hot—epically hot—and the mat baked under the sun. We all got terrible mat burn, but not from being dragged across the ring—just from taking bumps on a scalding surface. It felt like wrestling on a stove. If we hadn't been so head-over-heels in love with wrestling, that match might have been the moment when we called it. It just seemed so barbaric.

I remember at one event, waiting around in the church kitchen to go on. We had to keep cracking open the door to listen for our entrance music and would make eye contact with the ten fans out there every time—though I don't think they were fans, I think they were just confused church members. They certainly didn't know what to make of us when we came barreling out of that kitchen. They didn't boo, they just watched us, mouths agape. After matches, we'd roll over to Applebee's for drink specials, $5 wine, and cheap food—after all, we were making $500 a week, so every penny counted.

## Brie

Those matches were essential training. The stakes may have been low, but the circumstances were real. Wrestling gets a bad rap for being "scripted," but the reality is that inside that ring, a lot of it is improvised. Before you step out on the ramp, you know who needs to emerge victorious, but the voyage to that moment is often unplanned. In the early days, we would identify a few key "spots," or turning points—like when the babyface, aka the good guy, would begin to make their comeback against the heel. But the reality is that the more you have to memorize in terms of choreography, the more stress you inject into an already stressful situation. You can freeze—really go completely blank—if you're trying to recall a planned move or moment of choreography mid-match. If you're racing to get to move A, B, C, or D, then you don't have time to stop and think and react in the moment. Developmental was critical for learning how to get into the flow, to read each other's body, to learn how to talk to each other throughout the match.

## Nicole

I'll never forget my first singles match with Nattie soon after we got up to the main roster. I did a Lou Thesz press, which is a jumping straddle, and we accidentally hit heads so hard I totally lost my bearings. I just spaced, like a deer in headlights. We got up and then just stood there, staring at each other until I panicked and kicked her in the vagina, just because I knew I had to do *something*. You could hear the groans ricocheting throughout the stands as they felt her pain. When I got backstage, Vince pulled me aside and said, "We don't kick girls like that here." Fortunately, Nattie could not have been nicer about it, and we still laugh about it today.

The other reason that you don't want to over-choreograph a match in advance is that things change all the time—you might be told when you arrive that you have ten minutes for a live match, which is shortened to five right before you step out for your entrance music. Then as you get started, the ref might whisper after ninety seconds that it's time to "go home," meaning that the comeback needs to start immediately because the match has been shortened to two minutes without anyone officially telling you. The coaches in developmental put us through those paces. We learned how to become flexible, to move through the plot effortlessly and efficiently so we could still sell a great show to the audience despite a condensed timeline.

In developmental, you really see it all—I'll never forget when we had to wrestle at Daytona Beach for a bunch of bikers. They loved every second of the Divas action but harassed and cajoled the men. You can imagine the spectacle of the guys in their leathers and the guys in their tights. And then there was the time at the middle school, when the audience erupted in chants of "Spic! Spic! Spic!" That was fun! All the ups and downs and randomness only steeled us for the big event. We learned how to flow in the face of racism, audience hate, audience love, a switched script, and the fact that things just didn't always go our way or how we hoped they would turn out. Wrestling requires flexibility and a certain openness.

# Brie

Our early days in WWE were pretty brutal. While we'd certainly eaten some shit during our time in developmental back in FCW, the women on the main roster knew how to step it up a notch, as there was TV time and mainstage matches at stake. But we decided to just take it. A lot of girls wouldn't—they couldn't stand the hazing and bad treatment, and they would ultimately just bail. You really, really had to have a passion for wrestling and a love for the ring for it to feel worth it. But we just smiled, because we could tell that in WWE, there's no way around it, only through it. The backstage operates by tribal law. There are many unspoken rules enforced by other wrestlers. Depending on who has seniority, it can be really oppressive. It still boggles my mind that they wouldn't let us change in the locker room when we debuted, for example. Instead we had to change and get ready in the arena bathroom. That happened for the first few weeks, until the office caught us in there and told the girls they had to let us change in the locker room. It all felt really silly. Annoying, but at the end of the day, just stupid. And embarrassing if I'm honest. When you're new in a scene like that, you really just want to escape notice and fly under the radar. You don't want to be the focal point of everyone's hate and frustration. Honestly, though, neither FCW nor WWE was nearly as bad as what we'd been through in Arizona. And this time, we were in charge of our fates. They couldn't take away our smiles, or the fact that we were happy-go-lucky girls, thrilled to be away from bad memories, and thrilled to have our futures in our own hands. We weren't going to let anyone fuck that up for us.

And so we stuck to it. Nicole and I are really hard workers. We learned that from our dad. He may not have been perfect, but he knew how to put his back into it. He was a farmer—he managed a tree farm when we were young—and he always instilled in us that life is many things, but it is never easy. If you want something, you always have to work for it. Luck and opportunity are just by-products of hard work. We also knew how to be respectful and show deference to all the women wrestlers who had come before us and made our time there possible. What blew my mind, particularly at a place like WWE that is so character-driven, is that there was plenty of room for all of us. You know, I have a twin sister, who is as pretty and talented as I am—if anyone should have felt threatened, it should have been me. Growing up like that, constantly compared to Nicole, I know how ridiculous it is to feel competitive with other women. There were certainly a lot of battles for equality to be fought at WWE, and I understood why the women felt frustrated. Still, it seemed awfully silly to think that our battles should be with each other. By infighting and stepping all over each other, we were enforcing the cycle. We were all just keeping ourselves small.

The thing that was ultimately the most frustrating was that it wasn't clear what the other women were trying to accomplish.

Maybe they were trying to haze us to the extent that we'd give up and bail. We knew we needed to wait in line, that there were ten women ahead of us. But we also knew that no woman in the locker room had control over that line in the first place, since everything is dictated by management. I think that maybe that's why the women behaved so badly. They sniffed out scarcity, and felt completely powerless to control their own futures. It was easier to shit on us than to submit to their own powerlessness. I think they felt that they had to "do" something, even though there was really nothing to be done but work hard and hope for the best.

## Nicole

Besides the locker room bullshit, there are other rituals and rules at WWE that are easy to accidentally break, particularly because we didn't have anyone to really show us the ropes or tell us what to do. There is an unspoken rule, for example, that you must shake hands with everyone backstage and say hello. You can't walk past someone without doing this, even if they're deep in conversation. You're expected to sort of wait, awkwardly, until they finish talking and you can pay your respects. In the early days, we assumed we could circle back when people were free for conversation, because that seemed like the normal and noninvasive thing to do. But we learned quickly. The culture has evolved at WWE a lot since then. Thanks to the #MeToo movement, light is being thrown on how screwed up office culture is for so many women, regardless of industry. But as you can imagine, Brie and I were . . . upset. It was really scary to show up to work, as you felt like you could unknowingly mess up at every turn. We often felt like we were walking on eggshells. There were nonsensical rules and rituals that you could never fully know until someone was kind enough to initiate you. Let's just say that there was no formal onboarding process, and since we all work as independent contractors for WWE, there is no HR.

No matter the bullshit, you never went to the office—it just wasn't done. We were all expected to settle everything between ourselves. And sometimes that meant that a locker room meeting would be called against you. These were unofficial. I don't think the office even knew that this sort of thing happened, but a locker room meeting involved a number of female wrestlers marshaling against another wrestler. A year into our time on the main roster, there was a locker room meeting held against me, Brie, and Nattie. They were pissed at me and Brie for getting too much TV time. They were pissed at Nattie for being "annoying," though it was never made clear what that really meant. It was never clear to us what we were supposed to do about our TV time, which wasn't ours to control. They also felt like we had formed too many friendships with the guys. We liked hanging with them, particularly because there was way less drama. So we didn't feel like giving that up, either.

We took it, and put our heads down, and kept going. Due to my past, I've developed a high tolerance for bullshit—truly, nothing can break me. Brie and I both have a high tolerance for physical pain. The locker room stuff was annoying, and it made us dread going backstage, but it never got under our skin enough to make us want to give up. And when it came to the physical pain, that is just part of the game. Ultimately, the goal was to train to the point where you were a good enough wrestler that you wouldn't get injured, but that doesn't mean that you don't feel those moves, even when your adrenaline is doing its job to get you through it so you can get back on your feet. And getting back on your feet is key. You have to master the physical craft before you can learn how to tell actual stories with your body and elevate what's happening in the ring to a performance worth watching. (Honestly, at the beginning, you're just trying to get through it.)

I think one of the reasons that we made it through those early years was that we acknowledged how much we had to learn. We acknowledged that we were really green. We knew we had potential, but we also knew that we needed to go to school, as much as possible, to learn all that we could about wrestling. We never thought, "Oh, we've made it, the fans are into us, we're set." We knew that we needed to grow and evolve with the product. We couldn't rest on our laurels of having our niche, just because we were the first female identical twins to debut in WWE.

*Nicole*

For a long time, our shtick was Twin Magic, which is where one of us would hide under the ring to tag in halfway through the match for the win. It was fun for a long time, and the crowds loved it, but we wanted to develop as individuals, too. We were always pitching the producers and writers ideas for evolving the storyline because we wanted to push it and try new things. It became clear early on that at WWE you have to know how to fight both in and out of the ring. You have to be able to advocate for yourself, otherwise you're quickly swept into oblivion. This is not to say that advocating meant that anyone would listen. But you had to have one foot forward at all times, feeding them ideas to the point that they would rather deal with your storyline than listen to you any longer. Hey, perseverance pays off!

So, whenever we felt like it had been too long since we'd been on TV, we'd fight for a storyline to get back on. At one point, we hadn't been on TV for eleven weeks, which is danger-ously long—this was at a point when they would let wrestlers go seasonally. If they weren't using you, it could be quite ominous. So we hustled and pitched ourselves to assist the celebrity guest hosts. Bob Barker was on the schedule, so we asked Johnny Ace if we could accompany him as the Barker Beauties. Johnny thought it had potential, so he told us to go and pitch Vince. Bob Barker was amazing, and we pulled it off. This cemented a long run of accompanying the celebrities. WWE backstage is pretty overwhelming, so we would meet them when they arrived and give them a tour and make them feel comfortable. Hugh Jack-man, Kristen Wiig, a very stoned Snoop Dogg, Will Ferrell . . . it was really fun.

Next, we asked if we could have a storyline on *Superstars*. This was their C show, which they would record before *Live* would go live. It's not the best gig, but we figured if we were going to show up for work, we wanted to work—not just eat catering and hang out backstage. It was wrestling, it was a chance to get better and better, and it was a way to stay engaged even if they weren't ready to give us top billing. We respected all the women ahead of us, but we knew we wanted to take their spots and someday be the top women in WWE—and be ready for it. We knew it would take a long time, but we also knew that we could get there. We always felt like if we did it, we could make a difference and break barriers. And did I mention that I'm also really competitive? I don't like to lose.

## Brie

It was certainly cutthroat backstage, because there was a scarcity of opportunities for the women. There just weren't that many spots for us, and what were available were short (two minutes during TV events, max). It's hard to blame the other ladies for eye-rolling at the newcomers, for resenting the competition. I think we were all a little angry, and everyone felt powerless at that time to change things. I think everyone just needed to put their hurt and dismay somewhere. It was easiest to put it on the other female wrestlers. Because Nicole and I are identical twins, we saw things a bit differently. After all, we had to share a womb, and knew there was a way to share the stage with other women as well. We knew firsthand that multiple women can have success simultaneously. Nobody gets ahead when you screw people over and make them fail, particularly in a sport like wrestling where it was on all of us to make each other look good out there.

There were some hilarious times, too, particularly the late-night drives from town to town after the matches. We didn't have smartphones for a long time, and so we would have to print out reams of directions from MapQuest (it's still around, we've checked). And then we'd yell at each other. I might be scared to drive in snow, and scared of driving on big hills, but Nicole drives like she doesn't care if she dies. She's a nut behind the wheel.

Honestly, I was just so happy to be there. I had a fun and amazing job where I got to express myself through my body, where I was paid to travel the world and entertain crowds. I mean, pinch me, people! I got to go to Paris and fight in front of an arena. Making money was nice, but if I'd needed to, I would have paid the company for the privilege to do my job. I couldn't understand some of the misery that abounded backstage. People were so angry and so intent on screwing each other over. But it was clear that there were a million people who would have given their left nut to be in our positions. I had never been spoon-fed in life—I had always had to fight for it. I just don't think they realized how bad it could be. Bear had made me grateful. My grandfather, Pop Pop, made me grateful. I was intent on having the best time, even when some of the other wrestlers wished us nothing but ill.

*Nicole*

While we all wanted as much TV time as possible, the non-televised live events were far more fun. For one, the matches were significantly longer because you weren't capped by commercial breaks and run time. They were even less choreographed. During live events, you're able to create as you go. It's like any sport or craft, in that once you know what you're doing, you're able to perform at the next level. In wrestling, this means that you can get into the ring with your opponent and go with it—pushing each other to try new things. It's kind of like dancing, actually, if you have chemistry with another wrestler, if you know how to move with each other and communicate in the ring. If you're up against someone who is willing to work to make you look good by selling the bumps, then you can make some incredible matches, where the crowd feels every blow you take. It just takes practice. I still remember my first TV event. The referee, Scott Armstrong, just kept saying, "Breathe, baby girl, breathe."

Two of my favorite people to wrestle were Paige and Nattie—Paige because we took chances that other women wrestlers weren't taking at the time, and Nattie because we could go rough on each other and there were never any hard feelings. Nattie was always great to us. She came from wrestling royalty and had certainly done her time in developmental, but she didn't hold it against us. She was down in Florida at FCW with us, and we came up to the main roster at the same time. We taught her how to dress and look cute, but she taught us how to wrestle. Nattie has kept some of the costume pieces that we gave her from those early days because they remind her of our friendship, and also how people can be giving in an industry where many weren't that helpful. We really tried to empower each other—Nattie knew us when we couldn't wrestle at all, and she made us better. My most aggressive matches were always with her. I always loved wrestling Brie, too, because there was a trust between us that you can't create with someone who isn't your twin sister. I never had to worry that Brie's timing would be off, or that she wouldn't be there to catch my dives, or that we would go at each other too hard. When we had a storyline where I turned on her, I transformed into the meanest sister you can imagine. I got to be the sister on top, and I relished every moment.

In my early days, I probably learned the most from Beth Phoenix. She taught me how to communicate throughout the whole match in a way that the audience can't tell. When you're wrestling and working really collaboratively, you communicate constantly— sometimes during holds, or through the refs, or with our bodies. You have to be mind-locked into your opponent, to understand what they're going to do next and where you need to be to make it work for the audience—particularly if you haven't been involved in long storylines with each other, where you learn the way they move intimately. I always preferred wrestling women who were roughly my height, because it's just physically easier to get into it. But there is real artistry in wrestling against women who are taller, too. One tour, I was wrestling Tamina, our Samoan, who was the daughter of Jimmy "Superfly" Snuka, a famous wrestler. The goal was to make her look larger than life so that when I ultimately vanquished her, it would be like I had beat Goliath. I did the simplest stuff, but the crowd reacted like I had just won the World Cup. If you can be good at telling stories like that in the ring, you can be where The Rock is in his career. The physical moves make you, of course, but using your body to tell stories, to sell it to the crowd, to entertain them so they never want to watch anyone else, that's the real art form. That's what we were all trying to achieve.

# Brie

During our time in WWE, it was incredible to watch as the matches transformed and became increasingly athletic and intense. In the early days, they would search for athletic models who they could turn into wrestlers. I guess you'd liken it to the *Glow* experience, where you'd go to an audition and either take to the sport or not. But over the years, they started bringing on women who were athletes first, and it changed the nature of the matches.

Ultimately, other things started to change, too. Over the five years of our first WWE contract, the really bad apples started to get fired, one by one. The scene backstage became healthier, friendlier, and less intensely competitive. As we became veterans, we also vowed to change the culture, and to try to create more camaraderie among all the women. While the tendency is to still avoid going to the office for troubleshooting, people act like professionals in handling their backstage issues. Over the years, Nicole and I became leaders in the locker room. We worked hard to make it better, going out of our way to bring new wrestlers in under our wings. We had always taken care of each other, we had always been taught that you look out for other women. We might not be best friends outside of the building, but we were all sisters inside of it—and so it seemed only fair that we should make the whole scene a less oppressive experience. It was intimidating enough without the hazing, which seemed totally unnecessary. The women who came up either wanted to be there, worked hard, and showed respect—or they didn't. But it wasn't our job to enforce their behavior. People ultimately are who they are, and they will show you their true colors whether you force it out of them or not. We knew how to keep order, how to keep high-strung emotions under control. Ultimately, we just didn't want anyone to feel how we had felt when we first got to the main stage. Thank God we'd had each other.

## Nicole

This does not mean that we both behaved perfectly. In fact, stuff goes on backstage that's worthy of its own promo, whether it makes it to a storyline or not. I had a pretty big beef with another female wrestler for a number of years, which culminated in a heated argument. I can't say that I'm proud of it, but she had been telling stories about me backstage for years, and I finally had enough. I think her ex-boyfriend had a crush on me that triggered the whole thing, but her behavior became so ridiculous and hurtful that I decided to put a stop to it. I cornered her and gave her a three-minute speech about all the shit I had put up with in my life, culminating with: "I'm not the girl you fuck with." Brie had to pull me off her before I ripped her hair off her head and slapped her hard.

There weren't that many times that we lost our cool, despite all the instances that we felt like we had been unfairly messed with. I'll never forget one incident in the early days at FCW. In developmental, they put most of the logistics on the talent to execute. There was a lot of "Oh tell such-and-such wrestler this, or pass the word on to everyone." WWE was down in Tampa for *Monday Night Raw*. When they came to town, the FCW crew would gather so the producers could pull together impromptu matches and see how we were all coming along. One of the girls was supposed to pass on the call time to us, and she told us that we needed to be there at showtime, 7 p.m. It turned out that the call time was 2 p.m., and she just wanted us to fail. We were yelled at and humiliated. That was pretty typical of the type of shenanigans that went on.

We refused to let them get us down. Throughout our wrestling careers, it chafed people that we stayed positive and happy even when things were taken away from us. The other wrestlers couldn't understand, for example, how we were capable of having so much fun at a hotel bar when we weren't getting enough time on TV. But it seemed pretty obvious to us: We were being paid to wrestle, traveling the world, and life could have been much, much worse.

## Brie

There had been a lot of women in WWE who don't mind being a guy's valet and more or less leaving it at that. But we wanted stories that were also about women—that allowed us to express our individuality. And WWE wouldn't give those stories to us until we made them miss us by opting to leave when our contracts were up. When we came back, we came back with cameras. Finally the cameras were on women, telling women's stories. *Total Divas* was amazing for us for many reasons, but I think the most important factor for me and Nicole was that we got to show the audience who we were separately for the first time. It was at that time that WWE started letting us dress differently—they stopped making us be so twin-y.

When I could finally start dressing like me, I decided to integrate different types of plaid. From middle school up, I was a hippie little punk rocker who loved ska. I wanted to bring that out and show that side. So I wore flannel around my waist for a nineties grunge-y vibe. Meanwhile, Nicole's inspiration for her outfit came from her time playing competitive soccer (her soccer jersey number was 02), which you could see in her jersey top, backwards snapback, knee-high socks, and Nikes. It seems like such a small thing, but it was so liberating to be able to start to dress like ourselves. It gave voice to the little girls inside us.

As our storylines changed, our gear kept evolving, too. When Nicole was out with her broken neck and Bryan was out with a concussion, I got into a storyline against Charlotte Flair, and I started to wear their clothing. I brought in Bryan's kickpads and Nicole's shorts, just to inject the whole thing with a little more emotion, to heighten our matches with everything that I had at stake—because Nicole and Bryan couldn't be there to fight, too. People knew I had their gear, and they would look for it out there in the ring. In retrospect, it might not have been the right move, since Nicole's ass was significantly larger than mine. It wasn't my best look. But surprising, delighting, and changing it up are key—in wrestling, you always have to evolve, whether that means a new look or becoming a heel.

It's funny, because looking back at our early days in the ring, we were so far from sexy, particularly compared to the other women at that time, who were essentially pinups. I don't think we knew how to be sexy—we were PG, but I also think that it was a good thing. It made WWE a bit safer for younger girls who began to look to us as role models.

## Nicole

We have a really big female fan base, which is pretty incredible. WWE used to be entirely dominated by guys in the audience, but *Total Divas* has really helped women connect. They're going through the same stuff in their own lives as we are on the show, so they can relate on so many levels. Plus, they get to experience our lives as we live them, and there's something rewarding about that. They get to see us as ourselves, completely unfiltered. We've come to develop a really deep emotional connection with our fan base.

Brie and I were never judgmental people—we couldn't care less how the new girls who came into WWE got there. It was all about what they did when they arrived, and how they conducted themselves. As long as people were nice, respectful, and were working hard, we had no issue. It's funny, because a lot of people couldn't get over the fact that we didn't come from a wrestling lineage. We didn't spend years working in the independents, and our arrival in the ring wasn't sparked by our childhood dreams. Were they really expecting us to say no to an opportunity, or walk away, because we didn't have the same background as them? We never understood why the fact that we didn't have the passion at five meant we weren't entitled to have the passion for wrestling at twenty-one. That always blew our minds.

During the transition from the women being called Divas, to being recognized as Superstars just like the men, the women were really united. I believe that's why we made history—it took the whole locker room coming together. Obviously, the collective culture has shifted a lot, even just in the past few years, but one of the reasons that Brie and I decided to walk away from WWE was that we knew it had to change profoundly. We wanted equality, and we wanted respect. It took us leaving for everyone to realize that we were missed—that we actually brought a lot with us. It required coming back with cameras to really send the Divas Division—now Women's Division—to the next level (more on that later). The reality show was major for a number of reasons, but I think it was most impactful because people everywhere got to see how strong the women wrestlers really are. All on our own.

## *Brie*

One of the issues that Nicole and I have struggled with throughout our time at WWE is the concept of preferential treatment. And it didn't help when my mom married John Laurinaitis, aka Johnny Ace, the head of talent at WWE. I love Johnny. I loved Mom's second husband, Greg, too. He was such a sweet guy, and I was pretty devastated when it ended—but ultimately, they fell out of love, and were much better off as friends. When Johnny came into the picture, though, I knew she had finally met her match. We didn't set them up, and I had no idea that they were dating. I think they wanted to keep us out of it, to see if it was real before it became a thing. It's funny because when I found out about them, I was like, "When did this happen, and how could I have possibly not known about it?" WWE is pretty small.

They had known each other for a while because she represented us on a lot of our business deals—in fact, she came with us the first time we ever went to WWE. My mom runs a recruiting business, and she has always had a career to provide for our family. She has always been obsessed with business—and obsessed with guys who have a brain for it. She talks about work way too much, which made it hard for her when she was dating— nobody wanted a second date with her because she went on and on about the office. But Johnny loves to talk about business, too, and eventually they fell in love talking about contracts, equity stakes, and P&L statements. Really sexy stuff.

They're pretty much perfect for each other: They hang out in their sweats and ride their bikes to the pub so they can talk about business over beers. That's their best day ever. It was hard on us initially because our mother was effectively dating someone in management, even if he had no oversight over our careers. When news broke that they were involved, it definitely created more problems for us, and not in a trivial way. I could hear the whispers throughout the halls: "Oh now the Bellas' stepdad works in the office." By the time they got married, it had quieted down, but their relationship definitely spurred on the rumor that we always got favorable treatment.

We had learned that this would always come with the territory—nobody could accept or get comfortable with the idea that we had earned something for ourselves. Nicole dated one of the biggest wrestlers of all time, so our success is entirely because of him. Or I'm married to Daniel Bryan, so it must be that. Why is it so hard to believe that a woman can get something on her own? This sort of thinking, this trivial bullshit, is why women haven't had more opportunities in WWE—we keep ourselves small. That's why there are one hundred dudes, and fifteen women who are Superstars. Those numbers could and should be far more equal, and we left WWE when our five-year contract was up to help start a movement to prove exactly that. Meanwhile, Triple H was beginning a revolution with the women wrestlers at NXT that would push this issue front and center.

# CHAPTER 6

# BREAKING DOWN THE WALL

## 2012-2019

Land O' Lakes, Florida

San Diego, California

### Brie

In 2012, as our five-year contract at WWE was coming to an end, Nicole and I decided to leave. We were tired of pushing for storylines that weren't coming, and we wanted more TV time and longer matches. Essentially, we just wanted more equality. They had made it clear to us that they thought the twin thing was played out, but they rejected everything new we pitched. They didn't want to give us what we really desired, which was a shot at making it as solo wrestlers. Instead, they wanted to keep us in nonessential storylines where we were assisting celebrity hosts and fighting over the male wrestlers, which *we* thought was tired. It was a hard decision. We both really loved wrestling, but we decided it was time to go. We had come to a point where WWE was no longer helping us reach the next level. We had been talking to E! about doing a reality show about our extended farming family in Brawley, so we decided to pursue that as our next chapter.

The fans missed us, which was really gratifying. Shortly after we left, WWE reached out to us to broach the idea of having us stage a comeback. Separately they had been talking to E! about creating *Total Divas*, and E! wanted us to be in it. I think WWE knew we had never wanted to leave in the first place but that we were unhappy, and that they could get us to come back if they made the terms more fair. So we returned, with the E! cameras in tow. This was when *Total Divas*, a show about female wrestlers, both on the mat and off, was born. While backstage has historically been kayfabe, or else "behind the wall" and off-limits—important for the fans in terms of preserving the "reality" of the ring—the show idea was compelling to WWE. It promised to open up the sport and the network to legions of potential fans who had never thought that there might be something for them in wrestling. And in reality, kayfabe was gone—WWE was growing up and becoming more corporate. With that, it was no longer possible for them to insist that everyone maintain wrestling personas in their real lives. At that point they encouraged us to be ourselves, while also expressing that in the ring, we were "Broadway with body slams"—we were characters that were larger than life.

Bryan and I were in the early days of our relationship when Nicole and I decided to leave WWE. This certainly threw a wrench into the plan—it meant that we were no longer spending the majority of our weeks together traveling on the road as a couple. But I knew that if we were meant to be, we would figure out how to make it work, despite the distance. Staying in the ring simply to be close to Bryan wasn't how I had pledged to lead my life. This strength came from Bear: I couldn't make decisions based on anything other than what was right for me. Ultimately, it ended up being great for us.

Nicole and I got a lot of hate when we were filming the pilot. While many people at WWE wanted to be on the show, some wrestlers acted like they didn't want the cameras around and that we were sell-outs for going on reality TV. But that always rang pretty hollow—after all, we were all vying for TV time in our careers. We were all entertainers who wanted to draw the biggest crowds possible, and we were all tangling with the line between reality and entertainment already. So why wouldn't you want to do it for an even bigger audience and show the world how female wrestlers can kick ass? But it definitely kicked up stuff for us backstage, maybe just jealousy. It certainly didn't help that a lot of the Smart Marks, otherwise known as the know-it-all wrestling fans who know wrestling is choreographed but also hate when that fact is revealed, trolled wrestlers online who were doing the show, which only made it easier for other wrestlers to dump on us for not "being cool." Honestly, my feeling was that if they were going to live and die by the opinions of people on the internet, then they were going to die broke. People who weren't cast in the show would cover their faces when the cameras were rolling, I think just to make us feel awkward and foolish. It's ironic, because Bryan and I are quite private, shy even. But the opportunity seemed too good to turn down—not only have we gotten to show millions of people another side of professional wrestlers, but in our spin-off, *Total Bellas*, he has gotten to show off his composting toilet and gardening skills, too. If he introduced even one fan to environmentalism, or inspired even one person to use less water, then in his eyes, it was worth it. His heart truly bleeds green.

Nicole's boyfriend at the time agreed to do the show for her. They were in a new relationship, the producers didn't even know that they were dating when they started filming, and it felt weird for him to not be shown. Plus, he was really proud of her, and wanted to show up for her, even though he is extremely private. I think he also realized how important it could be for women's wrestling, for people who might not otherwise get involved with WWE, to see how athletic and wonderful the sport can be. He never earned a dollar from the E! franchise.

## *Nicole*

While showing off wrestling was always the main goal of the show, it was a major relief to let fans see our more normal human sides as well, particularly because Brie and I had only ever been part of twin storylines. With *Total Divas*, the fans got to see us for who we really are. They got to see that Brie and I may be identical twins, but we're actually really different. When the cameras were rolling, they got to see who we were in love, who we were when we were upset, or sad, or happy. We forged really significant connections with our fans because they got to see themselves in us. They became attached to who we are in real life and not just to the characters we embody when we are in the ring.

The first season of the show was magic, because when you've never filmed a reality show before, you're not as self-conscious about how you're going to look or how you might be portrayed. The first season really captured what it's like backstage, when everyone is fighting for TV time and good matches. When it aired and they saw themselves, some of the girls became anxious about appearing crazy or emotional. They started to resist the urge to be so competitive for fear that they wouldn't be able to control their images. I still love the show, and I'm fortunate to be an executive producer on it as well, but it's become more about our personal lives and less about the wrestling. I wish there was more ring time because I'm still blown away by what we all achieve out there.

The best part of the show, by far, has been the new fans that it has brought to women's wrestling. They are coming—to live events and also to watch our matches on TV. It has an impact, because the more people there are holding up signs for the women, the more likely the WWE is to give us main event matches. I know that when the Divas were wrestling on TV, whether at *Raw* or *SmackDown*, we pulled some really high ratings. It is encouraging that the male Superstars aren't the only ones who can put asses in seats. Through *Total Divas*, we proved that there is a massive appetite for women's wrestling. We have connected with the fans in real and powerful ways.

## *Brie*

One of the most gratifying parts of *Total Divas* for me has been to show many of the real friendships among us. We are champions for each other, first and foremost, and we wanted to show that on TV. It was also important to us that we give our fans an honest look at our lives, including the ups and downs. Bryan didn't ask the producers to edit out his depression, because he knows how many others struggle with the disease, and the roller coaster of Nicole's heartbreaking relationship was on full display. As much as wrestling is an individual sport, it's actually much more like soccer— you can't wrestle yourself, you can't carry a match based on your own awesome performance, you need your opponent to play along, to sell the bumps. When you know you are letting the other wrestler win, your intent out there should be to make her look as good as possible, to entertain the crowd with your pain, your anger, your lust for revenge. It just doesn't work if you make it all about you.

It's frustrating when there is strife within the ranks, when it feels like we're not all after the same goal, which to my mind has always been to elevate women's wrestling across the globe. To give more girls a chance for big matches on the main stage, to change the world one snapmare and bump at a time—to show that women can be sexy and strong, beautiful and smart. The internal criticism and derision of *Total Divas* within the WWE ranks was frustrating, too. We felt like we were giving female wrestlers a voice and bringing more and more people to the sport—but people backstage, and increasingly on promos, were getting on the mic and slamming us for only being reality stars. It was maddening. The show was nothing but a positive for the women at WWE—I'd challenge anyone to tell me one negative thing that *Total Divas* has done to the industry. After all, we are women wrestlers in a male-dominated business who are doing our best to kick ass. We are in relationships, we drive ourselves from town to town in the middle of the night, we fight like mad out there, and we get shit done.

One of my favorite matches of all time was against Nattie at *SummerSlam* in 2013, right after *Total Divas* premiered. We were enraged, particularly at the suggestion that we weren't really wrestlers. Nattie and I went out there that night filled with so much anger, and we put all that energy into the mat. That's when running knee became my signature thing, because people could feel the force of emotion behind it. (In its ultimate evolution, I would scream "Brie Mode!" and then run at the other wrestler and slam her with my knee.) They could feel how real it was to leave it all out there in the ring. Nattie and I were determined to make every fan in the stands know who the *Total Divas* were—and we wanted them to know that we could wrestle as well as, if not better than, any other Superstar out there.

Some of the Smart Mark fans were also pissed, because they felt like we ruined kayfabe. Vince had broken down that wall long before, and had fully bought into *Total Divas*, so that never seemed fair. People knew that wrestlers in long-standing rivalries were actually friends in real life, that storylines were a fabrication for the most part. We have social media and the paparazzi to thank for that. But some hardcore wrestling fans like to blame the breaking of kayfabe on us.

It was documented on *Total Divas*, but WWE marked a big cultural shift in 2016 when they stopped calling the women Divas and started calling them Superstars, which is what they call the men. This is something that we had all wanted for a long time. Generations of women before us had fought for it, too. To create drama and tension for fans, Triple H and his wrestlers cut promo after promo to make it appear that the women on the main roster were clinging to the title of Divas, that we were resisting the tidal wave of feminism that the women of NXT were bringing to WWE. While on the whole this storyline was great for the sport, it was a bummer to be on the other side. Nicole, in particular, was really upset.

*Nicole*

To give you full context, let's back up for a second. In February of 2015 there was a tag match between me, Brie, Paige, and Emma—and it lasted for twenty-nine seconds. Essentially, when we got into Gorilla that night, the timekeeper told us that our segment had been cut to a flat two minutes, including entrances. We had started out the day planning for eight minutes, which was then winnowed down to five. Two was ridiculous. We all looked at each other and just knew that we were going to stage a protest. We got in the ring, and without doing anything else, Brie put her finisher on Emma and ended the match. We knew that the fans would be furious, but we also felt like we needed to make a statement.

In wrestling, you can theoretically tell a story in sixty seconds—a minute can be a long time out there—but we were tired of the bullshit. There are sixteen segments in a show, and some matches go for two to three segments. On *Raw* that night, our two-minute fiasco was the only segment for women. It felt offensive to us that they hadn't trimmed one of the men's matches instead to give us a shot at doing something real out there.

The fans were outraged, and they started a tweetstorm with the hashtag #GiveDivasAChance. It was an incredible moment that we could all feel was coming for a long time—decades really—as the women were bringing more and more people to the sport. Fans naturally wanted to see us, and they were furious when they felt like we were short-changed, which honestly happened all the time. WWE knew that they needed to do something to address the fans' growing disillusionment.

I felt it marked a moment of change in the industry. But then it became a different sort of storyline. Paul Levesque, otherwise known as Triple H or Hunter, is Stephanie McMahon's husband.

She is the heir to the WWE throne—Hunter runs NXT, the developmental league, and he is incredible at crafting stories. A storyline emerged out of NXT that made it look like Brie and I, and the rest of the cast of *Total Divas*, were holding the women wrestlers back, rather than using our popularity and the general interest in the sport to push the whole thing forward. I get that it made good promos, and that WWE is predicated on drama and conflict, but this was so real to me. It was so important and central to what Brie and I, and many of the other Divas, wanted to accomplish there. It was ultimately upsetting.

We had been groomed to be Divas, and to make the audience, and all the girls who came to watch us wrestle, care about the Divas, and care about the Divas title. Then they groomed the NXT girls to give interviews mocking us and mocking the Divas. NXT claimed that WWE had hired Divas to be Divas, but that this next class of women were actually real wrestlers, ready to bring change. We were working our asses off, slamming our bodies and breaking our necks—literally. We were doing media all over the country to make people appreciate the word *Divas*, so that they could turn around and make it look like the women of NXT were leading a revolution?

I think what really bummed me out was that we were all fighting for equality and we were all supposed to be on the same side. But instead, in order to turn the transition into drama, they decided to split us up. That bothered me, to be positioned as the people who were holding women back. I had to continue to be reminded that it was just a storyline, and a way to bring up Charlotte, Becky Lynch, Bayley, and Sasha Banks. But after all that we had put on the line, it was hard to not take it personally.

I got a lot of texts from women who had helped to drive the sport forward over the years. In that NXT move, they all felt like their hard work never counted. Instead of being celebrated as part of a long lineage of change, it looked like they were bringing the inequality on themselves. We got to the point of being called Superstars because of the women who paved the road for us— it started with Mae Young, the Fabulous Moolah, Sensational Sherri, Luna Vachon, Leilani Kai, Alundra Blayze, Jacqueline, Trish Stratus, Lita, Torrie Wilson, Molly Holly, Victoria, Mickie James, Beth Phoenix, Gail Kim, Melina, Michelle McCool, Natalya, and so many more. We were part of different generations who all wanted the same thing—respect, more match and TV time, and to be taken seriously as wrestlers and athletes.

It was also frustrating because, plain and simple, it wasn't the truth. The NXT women were given the history-changing matches because they were the ones chosen to make history. And I guess that's kind of life. That is certainly wrestling, where perception is reality. (And to give full credit, they are incredible wrestlers. They were trained to wrestle in the way that a lot of women who came before them were not. They are Superstars.)

I didn't break my neck, and have my tits out, and get paid $500 a week to hang out with a bunch of male wrestlers. I wanted to be a top female Superstar in that company. I wanted to change how women in the sport were perceived. And I do believe that we have succeeded: We were the first women to be able to do all that

Brie and I have done in merchandise sales. And when those NXT girls came up, we wanted to help them look damn good. When Charlotte was the next big push, I got behind her 100 percent. I was the naughtiest girl, the baddest girl, the biggest villain so that Charlotte, as a babyface, ruled out there. I'm good at it, after all. I learned how to embrace being hated when I was a kid making my way around that soccer field.

*Brie*

This past decade at WWE has taught us a big lesson about the power of uniting for a cause. When I think about how we all came together, and how we then took over, I'm blown away by what we accomplished. It can be frustrating, and you don't get to tell your story exactly how you would like, or in a way that seems completely fair, but we have all had some incredible opportunities.

The other thing that seemed important to remember is that we were all supposed to be different—not cast from the same mold of what it means to be a female wrestler. Some girls are better wrestlers out there, some girls are better on the mic; some girls are better heels, others are better babyfaces. Everyone can be at a different level and it still works. It gives the show texture and makes it better. Ultimately, it's a beautiful thing. If you were to look at my record, you'd see I've probably lost more matches than I ever won. That was fine with me because it was always about the bigger show. Nicole and I became heels in our early storyline with Bryan, when I attacked Gail Kim for being his girl-friend. And we stayed heels, which means that more often than not, everyone is rooting against you. I had no problem putting over other women all the time. I was always grateful to be out there. It always seemed like it was about something bigger than my own personal glory. But in the industry, where perception is reality, our heel-dom probably did make fans believe that we weren't good people.

I was Divas Champion for a short period, probably about ninety days. I found out that it was going to be my turn when I was having dinner with my sister and some friends in Greenwich, Connecticut, just outside of New York. I got a text from one of the writers that they were going to give me a shot, and we imme-diately popped some champagne. I hadn't seen it coming and was blown away, as I didn't know if I would ever get that chance. I was a heel, after all, and we were really good at being bad girls. But it was time for a heel to get the title so that the babyfaces could chase it, which worked out for me. The creatives at WWE really do come up with strong stories that will be good for the title. Then they really do try to give every girl who has worked hard a chance to be the champ. I was thrilled. I took the title from Eve, and it was awesome. Before the match, she made the ref mark up Nicole's hand with a Sharpie so that we couldn't pull Twin Magic (we tried anyway).

The night I lost the championship, they were putting me against an opponent based on a fan vote. My boss told me that I would wrestle whomever the fans picked, and I wouldn't know who it was until showtime. It was between Eve Torres, Beth Phoenix, and Kelly Kelly. They each wanted to put together the outlines of a match, and so I had to memorize all three. I stood out there in the ring, running through moves, waiting, hoping I wouldn't forget or get the spots confused. Ultimately, I lost to Kelly Kelly after she pinned me when we were doing a double somersault.

The thing about wrestling is that it really is a team sport with an individual champion. We don't all get to be that champion at the same time. Someone's going to be on top, and for the rest of us, that means it is not our turn. But it's much better for all of us when we take turns and help the girl who is the champion stay up there for as long as possible. When we work as a team, everyone is more into it. The audience can feel our collective energy, can get into the momentum of the matches and the emotions we're projecting. You can't be compelling when you're not working together. It's just a fact. And you can't be compelling if you're not driven by passion.

Nicole and I have always had passion in spades. The more people tell us that we can't do something, the more jacked up that passion gets, and the more inclined we are to prove them wrong. We turn as many nos into yeses as we can. We have become expert at transforming hate into gold. A lot of people at WWE wanted our reality show to fail. Well, we've turned it into a multi-season hit with a hit spin-off. A lot of people told Nicole that she'd never be champion. Well, she became the longest-reigning Divas Champion ever . . . and she'll never lose that record now that the title is retired. That resilience and drive is everything, particularly when it's paired with positivity—it's a combination that just can't lose. When you see the world for its bright spots, negativity is just not part of its definition.

## Nicole

While Brie and I have gotten ourselves really far on grit and determination, we wouldn't have our life without Vince McMahon. He has given us opportunities consistently and constantly—and that's why WWE will always be home. I would never turn my back on the people who have made me. Vince invented the Bella Twins, and Brie and I will always be grateful for that.

We weren't alone, nor were we singled out for special treatment. Vince gives everyone an opportunity—everyone who comes down that ramp gets a chance. He can't control whether the crowd connects, he can only give you the blank canvas, the ring, millions of eyeballs, and then it's up to you to do something with it and turn it into a career. I grabbed that canvas and painted a Picasso. I knew I wouldn't stop out there until I could be on top.

He isn't shown on *Total Divas*, but within WWE, Vince has an open-door policy. He always wants people to come to him for advice. If you don't understand a storyline, or it seems backwards, he'll walk you through how he envisions it moving you forward. He's a brilliant strategist and storyteller. For example, when I was a week away from being the longest-reigning champion, he sent

Brie out to wrestle in my stead. And she was beaten. The crowd freaked out because they thought I had lost, and they started booing like crazy. Then, Brie slowly started pulling tissues out of her bra to reveal that it was her and not me that had lost. That was Vince's call. I was skeptical about whether it would work, and it turned out to be epic.

We've gotten to travel the world on his dime, we've built the Bella Army under his careful watch, and most important, we've been able to be intimate with and connect to millions of strangers, who have truly come to be like real family and friends. Brie met the love of her life and went on to make another love of her life. We have built an incredible career that allows us to help others and give back. How lucky are we?

*Brie*

Stephanie McMahon, Vince's daughter, who is the Chief Brand Officer at the company, is an incredible role model for the women of WWE as well. She was a wrestler, so she understands what it's like out there. She has played a central role in fighting for more equality and parity for all of us. As part of "The Authority," together with her real-life husband, Triple H, she has also played a central role in my storyline, because of a long-standing feud with Bryan, aka Daniel Bryan. When Bryan was going to be "fired" by Stephanie in the storyline, I stepped up to her. This culminated in a lot of hilarity and drama until she came out of retirement and we ended up wrestling against each other in *SummerSlam*.

So this is how our path to *SummerSlam* went down: I obviously never pitched or asked for this storyline, because Stephanie is my boss, and asking to wrestle her would have been an insane thing to do. But it happened organically—and miraculously, she was game to do it, which was incredibly generous. In fact, it was her idea. The whole spectacle kicked off when she slapped Bryan. Now, if we had still been in the Attitude Era of the nineties, he would have just slapped her back, or put his finisher on her, but he had to stand there and take it across the face. The only person who could step in and respond in kind to stop her was me.

Bryan and his "Yes!" chant led the opposition against "The Authority." In fact, in an incredible moment, there was an Occupy WWE movement where hundreds of people wore Daniel Bryan T-shirts and protested against "the man" by sitting ringside. Bryan represented the people. Bryan had broken his neck and couldn't wrestle, and so The Authority—i.e., Stephanie and Triple H— demanded that he give up his title while he was out recovering. The fans revolted, and so The Authority said that if he didn't give up his title, I had to quit wrestling. Bryan responded that of course I wasn't going to quit, and then right before he went to give up his title, I yelled, "I quit!" and slapped Stephanie McMahon.

The storyline went back and forth for a while, where we had each other arrested for assault (she and Triple H attacked me and Nicole when we were signing our contracts), and then we had our big, final confrontation where I told her I wouldn't press charges if she would wrestle me at *SummerSlam*. We had no time to go over the promo in advance and were quickly talking through the plan in Gorilla—where Vince McMahon, Triple H, your producer, and the timekeeper all sit—when her entrance music hit. It was a "Wait, what?" moment, and I just looked at Bryan, whose response was "Oh shit." We would have to wing it.

It all went off perfectly, considering that we were pretty much improvising out there. I knew I was going to throw down the challenge, and that she would accept it, but I still wasn't sure that we would actually end up wrestling. It was amazing to be in a storyline with Stephanie, and I learned so much from just interacting with her in promos. She taught me how to engage, how to hold myself with confidence, how to project like a powerful woman. She knew how to poke me and agitate me and ultimately motivate me to deliver performances that felt inspired and real. I will always be so grateful for that, because I was just some chick on the roster. She didn't have to put me over like that or share so much screen time with me.

Before our match at *SummerSlam*, we rehearsed together at the Performance Center. Stephanie and Triple H both helped me figure out the psychology of what we would need to do out there. They helped me put the moves to the emotion, to bring the crowd along in my rage against Stephanie and all that she represented. The best part was Nicole's role in the encounter, and the way that she turned on me at the last second to help Stephanie win. The crowd reaction was huge, which led to my second favorite match ever, which was taking on Nicole at the *Hell in a Cell* event. (The backstory of Nicole's betrayal is that when I "quit," Stephanie took out her vengeance on Nicole and put her in a string of handicap 4-on-1 matches where she was ripped apart by the other women, so Nicole was furious at me for putting myself first and abandoning her.) After my *SummerSlam* match with Stephanie, and my ultimate match with Nicole, Vince turned to me and told me that it should have been the main event. It was pretty fantastic.

## Nicole

We've had a lot of incredible matches, particularly because women's wrestling has evolved dramatically even in the past five years. When we first debuted on the main stage, there were a lot of things that we weren't allowed to try. The producers didn't really want women to do big moves, and a lot of the other women weren't interested in pushing for it, because they didn't want to take those bumps. They can hurt more, and they can certainly be more dangerous. In developmental I had done a lot of *lucha libre*, which is a bit more aggressive than what was being done on the main stage. I struggled to find wrestlers who wanted to play ball. They were worried about getting hurt or wanted to stick with routine stuff that they were familiar with. It was hard to find partners willing to push it.

That's why I loved wrestling Nattie and Paige so much—they were both so amazing about taking it and then giving it back. Like me and Brie, they would do anything to put on a good match, to elevate the sport to the next level. Paige and I both broke our necks, ultimately—and for her it has meant retirement—but in retrospect it still seemed worth it.

Because of how limited the segments were for the women, and because we didn't have much time out there when we did get storylines, it really mattered that we all got behind each other in the locker room. It often felt like a two-steps-forward, one-step-back proposition. I remember one event where Nattie and Brie had a four-minute match but needed to make room for a third wrestler to come out and cut a promo as she would be entering the storyline. I was Brie's valet. They decided to make the match short, at just two minutes, in order to give this third wrestler plenty of time to do her thing on the mic and get the crowd excited. Well, she didn't do that, and instead used the time to go on and on about herself and our "daddy issues." All of the *Total Divas* were furious in the moment because it was the exact reason why women weren't doing well in WWE—it was far too typical of how things went down. One woman wanting to outshine everyone else instead of connecting with the other wrestlers and the story we were set to do together. She was going into business by herself, which ruins any chance of building something as a team. If they had known, Nattie and Brie would have wrestled for the full four minutes and cut her out, but that's not how we ever chose to roll.

Backstage, Brie pulled her aside: "We're all in this together. You can have jealousy, you can have dislike, but the only way this

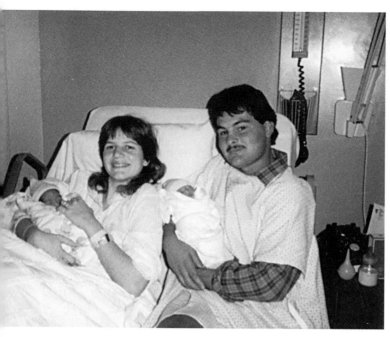

The day we were born at Mercy Hospital in
San Diego, California, on November 21, 1983.

In our bassinets at my grandparents' condo in
Scottsdale, Arizona, four days after we were born.

Pop Pop with us in 1984 at his condo in Scottsdale.

Nana with Brianna at my mom's baby shower in El Centro, California, in 1984. My mom missed her baby shower because we came early.

Hanging out at our grandparents' house in 1987.
Brianna is on the left and Nicole is on the right.

Us always looking so identical!!!
Brianna is on the left and Nicole
is on the right in 1992.

JJ and Nicole on a tractor in the Majesty fields in Brawley, California, in 1992.

Pop Pop with Nikki and Brie after our first communion in Brawley, California, in 1991. Brianna is on the right and Nicole is on the left.

Mutton Bustin' competition at the Cattle Call Rodeo in Brawley, California, in 1992. Nicole won!! Brianna on the left, Nicole in the middle, and JJ on the right.

Our parents in 1991 at the Garth Brooks concert in El Centro, California.

One of our favorite family vacations in Colorado at a dude ranch in 1990.

At our grandparents' house in Brawley, California, in 2003 for Drummer Boy Dinner.

Bear drew his and my split faces in 2001. He had them hanging
in his room, where they touched and created one face.

BEAR and BRI

A collage I made when Bear and I were together,
which I had on my wall by my bed in 2002.

Nikki and Brie making their entrance at *Wrestlemania* 31.

Brie hits a missile dropkick.

Nikki hits a spinebuster on Paige at *Wrestlemania* 31.

Brie versus Stephanie McMahon at *SummerSlam* 2014.

The night the women's *Evolution* began.

Main event of the first-ever pay-per-view all-women's WWE *Evolution* against Ronda Rousey for *Raw* Women's Championship.

John and Nikki in the
ring at *Wrestlemania 33*.

After so many years of blood, sweat, and tears, we finally got to walk down that iconic *Wrestlemania* ramp together as sisters, as champions.

Nikki, Brie, Emma, and Paige in-ring the night of Give Divas a Chance, February 23, 2015.

When Nikki became the longest-reigning Divas champion.

Brie and Bryan's wedding picture in Sedona, Arizona, at L'Auberge.
*Photo by Patrick J. Corley.*

Bryan and Birdie at her first swim class in San Diego, California, in 2017.

Birdie and Brie at our Phoenix home.
*Courtesy of Whitney DiNota of Whitney B Photography and* Paradise Valley Lifestyle.

division is going to grow is if we connect and put that other stuff aside. We have to stop stabbing each other in the back." I have no clue if it resonated. Change was always slow to come.

## Brie

It's funny to exist in the world of WWE because it seems like a fair number of wrestlers start to believe their own hype and start to believe their own storylines. It felt sometimes like we needed to constantly remind some of the women that we were creating fiction—that it wasn't real. (And that if we were to get into a legit fight, I'd kick their ass.) I wanted to shake some of the women sometimes and plead with them to just focus on building a really great storyline. It can seem real, it can totally be badass, but if we don't all work together, it's just stupid. Bryan and I would talk about that all the time on long drives between matches, that there were just too many people who believed in their own gimmicks. They got a little bit of fame— wrestling fame not George Clooney fame—and it all went to their head.

I think without all the restrictions—both on the time we had, and what we were allowed to do—the women could have just relaxed into it a bit more. I remember walking down the ramp during *WrestleMania* for a tag match with Nicole against AJ and Paige. It was a really memorable moment and an honor to walk down the ramp for wrestling's biggest event. We all wanted to do more in the match but weren't allowed to at the time, despite our best efforts to push beyond the line. At that point, they still wanted to reserve the big moves for the guys. Now there are really no limits on what we can get up to, which makes perfect sense to me. I think they were reticent to let us off the leash because they wanted us to seem feminine, but the reality is that many of us are thicker than some of the guys out there.

We are now many seasons in on *Total Divas*, but filming the show never gets old. It keeps evolving as our own lives morph and change, and being able to make *Total Bellas* with our extended family is a dream. I get to go to work with Birdie and my mom and brother and do fun things and get paid for it. It's certainly hard work, and when the cameras are on us it is relentless and the days are long, but I wouldn't trade it for anything. I will keep filming for as long as the viewers are interested. I get paid to go to Napa and get drunk with my sister. It doesn't get better.

The reason it's also worked for us for so long is that there isn't an expectation that we'll stoke drama—we just don't have to fabricate or fake it. As you can tell from these pages, which are full of stories we've never even told on TV before, there's plenty of drama without us even trying to stir the pot, and that's not taking into account the other women of WWE. When you take a bunch of very physical and dramatic women, and they're on the road for five days a week fighting for a living, shit gets real. That's just how women in WWE are. But we can step away and create some distance and all have beers together a few hours later. The fiery temperament that Nicole and I share is not dissimilar from how many of the female wrestlers operate. It has to be something that's in our collective blood.

The same goes for *Total Bellas*, which we film with our mom, and JJ, and Johnny, and JJ's wife, Lauren. As you know by now, we are quick to battle and fight in our family, and there are times when it certainly doesn't feel worth it. Just the other week we were filming, and Lauren was talking about her blog, and I mentioned something about the rules of recycling, and JJ jumped down my throat. It can be a lot, and it's tough to relive it again when the show airs because it can stir up old grievances.

My family has sacrificed a lot for the show, though I know that it will ultimately be worth it. When we filmed *Total Divas*, we didn't make much money at first, as it was all just for a pilot. But we knew it had the legs to potentially go far, and we had a lot of faith in it. I hope *Total Bellas* does for our family what *Total Divas* did for me and Nicole.

# CHAPTER 7

# HARD BUMPS

*2004–2018*

Los Angeles, California

Tampa, Florida

*Brie*

I never expected to be a stepmom when I was twenty-one years old, but when I met Craig, it seemed like a foregone conclusion. He had a seven-year-old daughter, who I loved. But I barely knew how to take care of myself, much less step in and be a role model for a second-grader. For whatever reason, I think because I was so blindingly in love, I thought I could figure it out—I was even willing to swallow the reality that when you're involved with someone who has kids, you have no shot of ever being number one in their heart. At the time, I thought I could change that—now that I have Birdie, I realize I had no shot.

I loved that little girl, though. And I really loved Craig, in a way that made it seem impossible that he wouldn't turn out to be the one. He really loved and cared for me and taught me some of the basics of life—in addition to being gorgeous, with blue eyes and long black hair and tattoos. He took me around the world and spoiled me. He made me feel like his girl, he made me feel special. I was young when we met, full of passion and a taste for drama, with a real desire to please. Craig was more removed—he loved me, and he wanted me to be around, but he also wanted his life to be as it was. Probably because of this, he always made me feel like I was really needy—and, as a side effect of that, a little crazy. Looking back, the tendency for guys to label women like that does, in fact, drive me crazy—actually, it makes me furious. I don't think there's anything strange about wanting a text from your boyfriend that says, for example, that he's landed safely after flying across the globe. I wanted those sorts of check-ins. I didn't think it was crazy to expect him to text or call to say good night if we were sleeping in separate states. It was a little ironic when this free-spirited, don't-tie-me-down-with-your-feelings-and-your-neediness hard rocker was really bothered when I moved to Tampa to pursue WWE.

I wasn't in Florida when Nicole broke her nose at FCW, because Craig had given me an ultimatum. I had been at a movie with friends when he sent me a text. It said he hadn't signed up for a relationship where I wasn't there to sleep next to him at night. I remember sitting in the parking lot outside of the theater and staring at my phone in a panic. He told me that if I didn't come back home, that was it, we were done. I was in love with

Craig, but I was also in love with wrestling. It was a tug-of-war for my heart, and it seemed unfair that he expected me to choose. I called the head of talent and begged for a bit of time off to go back to Los Angeles to make my relationship right. It seemed only fair that I work on it as hard as I was working on my wrestling. I thought I was going to get fired. People didn't really take personal breaks like that, however short it may have been, particularly when they were right on the cusp of potentially getting a shot at the main roster. Nicole was furious with me, as she had every right to be, for risking it. After all, her relationship with Jake had hit the shitter because of wrestling, and our chances for making it to the next level were handcuffed together because of our twindom.

Craig was used to being my number one without any sacrifice on his part. I didn't really know what to do with his dismay over feeling abandoned. He made me feel like I had left him behind in L.A. to rot. I took responsibility and felt like I was a bad person because of it. From his point of view, we had been attached at the hip for two years, and then suddenly he was expected to go to bed alone every night. At the time—and it frustrates me in retrospect—my point of view was that his point of view was right: I was disappointing him, and he had every right to feel angry with me. In retrospect, the writing was on the wall that our relationship had been, and always would be, uneven. There was an unspoken expectation that I would make all the sacrifices. After all, he only bothered to come and see me in Tampa once—and I had to buy his plane ticket on my measly salary. (To add insult to injury, there was only a direct flight to Orlando, and he refused to make a connection, so I had to drive and pick him up there.) It's funny, because he came to one of my matches at a bar named Bourbon Street, and he got emotional as he watched me wrestle. He was blown away and couldn't stop talking about it. When he had first met me, I was a waitress with some aspirations of becoming an actress. Then I had moved to Florida and morphed into a powerful athlete and entertainer. Based on that, I thought he would become more supportive. But he couldn't reconcile my absence with how he expected and wanted his life to be.

Once Nicole and I made it to the main roster, I was out on the road for four or five days a week. Then I would boomerang back to Los Angeles, trying to keep my relationship with Craig on the rails. I think because of our age difference, I was too intimidated to be honest about my emotional needs, and so I let him walk all over me. I don't think that was his intent; I just never challenged it. I didn't give myself permission to ask for what I wanted, like true intimacy, and freedom to pursue my own career, and ultimately, marriage and kids. I think that's why it was so confusing and disorienting to him when I initially moved to Florida—he took my constant presence for granted and assumed that our relationship was feast enough for my soul, that he was giving me everything I wanted, because I had never asked for more.

Over the next few years, as I traveled back and forth to Los Angeles, it started to feel really different. Distance can do that for sure, but I think I had also begun to learn how to express myself in the ring. Pretending like pleasing him was my primary goal in life just didn't sit right with who I knew I was as a person. I guess I was becoming myself: a firebrand, a loudmouth, a strong woman who speaks whatever is on her mind. I didn't want to believe that things had shifted between us; I was so in love with him and felt like I singularly held the responsibility for fucking it up. He was an awesome guy, and for a long time, we had an amazing relationship, and so much fun together. But I knew that I couldn't live only for a man. I needed to go and do what I was drawn to—I've always had Bear's voice in my head pushing me forward. I felt Bear's insistence in every fiber of my being, that I keep pushing it in the wrestling ring.

The fourteen-year age difference was hard. I was young and crazy and wild, and he was coming to the end of wanting to be wild and crazy. When he hit forty, I was only twenty-six—we were in totally different periods of our lives. I wanted to party and do crazy stuff, and it wasn't in the cards for him anymore. He'd had his fill. By the end, we were operating a bit like roommates. We still had a lot of fun together, drinking beers at the pub down the street, but we were really just friends.

Our relationship had been on the decline for a couple of years. During what would be our final June together, I gave my-self until Labor Day to turn things around. I figured if things changed, I'd stick around. But if things stayed as they were, I just couldn't do it. One breath, he'd want to have kids and get married; the next breath, not so much. I knew that marriage and kids were nonnegotiable for me, that my life wouldn't be complete without both. Then one day, I overheard him telling his friend Brett that he really just didn't want it. I was in the other room, and he didn't think that I could hear. My heart sank. I knew I wasn't in the business of trying to force someone into wanting something that they ultimately didn't want. I could hear in his voice that it was how he really felt, and that he just didn't have the heart to let me down. We had both invested almost five years in being with each other, and it was a lot to walk away from. So often, relationships come to feel like investments, and that they're somehow worthless if you don't fully cash out. You end up clinging to them for way too long. I knew it was time for us to let each other go. A few months later, I watched *Shopgirl*, the L.A.-based movie with Claire Danes (glove salesclerk) and Steve Martin (rich tech guy) and their messed-up love story. In it, her character acknowledges as she walks away from their one-sided relationship: "I can either hurt now, or hurt later." And I thought, "Wow, that's so true." I saw a lot of my own relationship in their dynamic. I knew I needed to start my crying now.

I called Nicole and asked her to come to Los Angeles with a U-Haul. Then I told Craig that I just couldn't do it anymore. He looked at me, and he knew in his heart that I was right—we cared about each other deeply, but we were falling out of love. I knew there was something better for both of us. I think he was blown away that I actually had the balls to leave, that I went through with it.

I put my stuff in storage, packed five boxes, and moved to the guest room of a good friend in New York City. Craig was like a father figure in many ways, which always made me feel young. But New York made me feel all grown-up—New York made me feel like a woman.

## Nicole

While Brie was living in Los Angeles trying to make it work with Craig, I was living in San Diego. I was wrestling during the week, while fighting my own relationship battles. As discussed, I have never been good at staying single—being alone is just not my natural, or preferred, state. But after Jake, I refused to jump into another relationship. And then, of course, because some lessons are really hard to learn the first, second, or third time, I involved myself with another playboy.

We can call this wrestler Brad. He was loud, and hilarious, and loved attention. After matches, we would all end up at the hotel bar, and he was always there to make everyone laugh, with a smart-ass joke for every occasion. He would look at me in a certain way, knowing that it would make me feel a certain way—he knew exactly what he was doing. He teased me a lot, too, the way you tease a girl you like in third grade. And he would make himself challenging—every girl loves a challenge. So I guess what I'm trying to say is that Brad knew how to hook a girl. And then mind-fuck her.

We started sleeping together, though that did not deter him from openly and aggressively flirting with other girls. Our relationship was casual, and I certainly had no claims on him, but it drove me crazy anyway. It was the first time that I had been with a guy who wasn't clamoring to lock me down. It drove me batshit crazy. It made me obsessed with him. The problem with that sort of imbalance is that it never really gives you a chance to assess the relationship, or your compatibility, on stable ground. You spend so much energy trying to get something that you think you want, that is just a little out of reach, that you don't have a chance to actually judge whether you want the thing in the first place.

I loved having sex with him, which only complicated matters. We had great chemistry in the bedroom, and he was still making me laugh. But he was a little cruel, too. He thought very little about protecting my feelings. I think he thrived on that gray area, that middle ground, where I was constantly left questioning the boundaries of our relationship with a big "What the hell are we?"

And then we had a really good year together where we settled into what felt like an adult relationship. We didn't tell each other that we loved each other, we rarely held hands, but it felt like we were together—at least while we were on the road with WWE. We were both living in Tampa at the time; he was toying with the idea of moving back to the Midwest, while I had decided to move back to San Diego. Because you spend a majority of your week together on the road when you're dating another wrestler, the geography of your permanent home doesn't really matter.

You're rarely there—if anything, you're relieved to have a bit of a break from each other during the off days. He was over at my apartment helping me pack, which meant that he spent the day playing around on my computer while I put stuff in boxes. When he headed home that night, he left his Myspace open.

Now, I know the rule. The second you start looking at something not intended for your eyes, you're probably going to find something that you don't want to see. But I couldn't help myself from scrolling through his messages. I didn't see anything out of the ordinary and was feeling ashamed for being nosy, when I decided to look at one more page. And then I saw messages from her: "Last night was so good." I kept scrolling and reading: Lies about me, bashing me, nude photos, endless flirtation. Then I saw where it started: "Last night was so amazing. I can't believe it finally happened." The messages were from one of my closest friends at WWE—a girl who had come to San Diego to see my family with me two nights before she apparently banged my man for the first time.

I called him and asked him to come back over and then slapped him hard. Then I started to bawl, because I would have never, ever done that to him. It was beyond hurtful, beyond the limits of the heavy and incessant flirting he did with other women on the regular, which already felt like it was boundary stretching for a healthy relationship. While we had never had a commitment talk, and I'm sure he had plenty of side pieces over the course of our relationship, there was a rule that was so sacred it didn't even need to be spoken: We did not sleep with other wrestlers. Not only had he slept with another wrestler, but he had slept with a wrestler who happened to be one of my closest friends, who knew about my feelings for him. It was an undeniable betrayal. I used to go out to dinner with both of them, while this whole drama was unfolding behind my back. He claims it only happened once or twice—but even that was two times too many. She called me repeatedly and left voicemails, but we never spoke again.

Fortunately, that was enough to end what was a dysfunctional relationship. It was fun while it lasted, and he is a friend to this day. But we had no business trying to make it work romantically. It's funny, because we always had such a great time together—I still love talking to him—but his fear of commitment, or just asshole-like tendencies, made it all so terrible. He legit made me feel like a stupid girl.

I rinsed off my relationship with Brad with a bartender in L.A., who was trying to make it in the industry. He was tall, dark, good-looking, hilarious—but as much as I liked him, our relationship was short-lived because it turned out he had a girlfriend. I was bummed and disappointed, but I was also used to shenanigans like that. And he did me the favor of breaking my cycle with Brad and giving it some finality and resolution. The bartender provided enough of a distraction for me, enough of a wedge, that I was able to quit Brad cold turkey instead of falling into an ongoing cycle of sleeping with him on and off depending on when I felt lonely. Brad will always make me laugh—he's an amazing guy. And it seems like he's finally ready to be a great husband . . . to someone else.

## Brie

Birdie and Bryan are hard to top, but the two years that I lived by myself in New York were some of my best. It was the first time in my life when I felt truly independent, financially stable, and had the luxury of really only worrying or thinking about myself. I didn't have a serious boyfriend who had a stake in my comings and goings, or a say over my schedule. There was nobody who held dominion over my emotions or could make me feel alternately good and bad. It was really liberating and really fun. I had a job I loved, I was making good money, I had made a little name for myself at that point. The city felt like it was mine to conquer. New York gave me other gifts, too, like the chance to tap into a life of arts and culture that I had first shared with Bear. I went to Broadway plays, I gallery hopped in Chelsea on the weekends, and hung out with musicians and artists. I even called my mother to tell her I was done with the West Coast for good.

Like Nicole, I was rebounding with bartenders across the city. Wrestlers and bartenders are, by nature, deeply compatible. Bartenders kept the same schedule as us, they gave us free drinks, and they took no issue with our itinerant lifestyle. When I was in New York City, it typically meant that I didn't have to work. I could party with them all night, and then sleep in all day. Some days I was in town; others, not. It was no-strings-attached, let's-use-each-other-for-drinks-and-sex fun. I felt like Carrie Bradshaw.

I moved into my own apartment just north of Soho in Greenwich Village—a sweet little studio with a big closet and a tiny kitchen (the fridge door would slam into the oven, which wasn't that problematic because I didn't keep anything in my fridge except for wine). It was the first time that I had actually lived by myself, and I relished every moment of it. I went to the nearby hardware store and painted the walls; I hung rock 'n' roll pictures that I put in distressed frames. It was a cute, little, shabby chic, rock 'n' roll joint, and it was all mine. I had a single big-ticket item on the wall, a guitar signed by Keith Richards, Pete Townsend, and Bruce Springsteen that I had drunkenly bid on at an auction. It was the most expensive thing I ever bought, but I still don't regret it.

I had made a pact with myself to stay single, to stay open to possibility, which popped up in spades throughout the city. It was a great time to be in New York—and maybe the city's still the same—but it felt like the chance encounters of living among millions of strangers meant that you could spark a romance on the subway, or at the very least a story that you could dine out on for a long time to come. It was also a great place to keep my pact of staying single, because it never seemed to me like anyone in New York City was actually looking for a real relationship. In fact, my very first date came shortly after I moved, when I got lost on the subway. This handsome Italian-looking man, in a nice coat and scarf and gloves, offered to help me find my way. He stopped his own journey home and escorted me to where I was trying to go.

I was totally charmed, and then he asked me to go to dinner. He took me to a really nice restaurant, where he started venting to me about his wife and kids. It was one of those record-scratch-to-silence moments. "Wait, you have a wife and kids?"

"Yes," he said. "But they live outside the city." I guess he thought that would put me at ease, and that propositioning me over dinner was a perfectly normal thing to do. He was looking for a Thursday girl.

"Do you think I look like the type of woman who wants to be your Thursday girl?" He seemed legitimately confused that I wasn't interested in his offer. It was a good reminder of why I had decided to stick to bartenders—sweet and uncomplicated. A short while later, I met a French guy who was my age. We started talking in the aisle at Whole Foods and he invited me over to his place in the East Village for a barbecue. We hung out for three straight days—and then he told me he had to go back to Paris, left, and to my knowledge, never came back.

Maybe it was Bear, but I always felt protected, even though I arguably did some dubious stuff (like going to random French guys' apartments in the East Village). I just pray that Birdie uses better judgment. But I also, admittedly, knew how to protect myself and would have quickly let my fists fly if I ever felt like I had gotten myself into a bad situation. And New York certainly taught me how to use my voice. I had always been tough, but more in a physical sense—living in New York gave me a verbal backbone and the confidence to speak my mind.

# Nicole

I got the WWE nickname "Fearless Nikki" because I took on a series of handicap matches after Brie "quit" to eventually go into a storyline with Stephanie. To feed it, Stephanie kept putting me in the ring against four or so other girls, which obviously resulted in a thrashing—but I kept taking it. In reality, I think it fits me, because there's not much that I won't do physically. Which is how I ended up with an *almost* broken neck. They say it's broken, but technically it's not fully there—it's an extreme herniation that stopped spinal fluid from reaching my C6 and my C7 vertebrae. It's so herniated that a piece was about to push through my spinal cord, which would have resulted in paralysis or death.

I think it all started when I did a match where I was thrown into the stairs in 2015. During moves like that, the crew is supposed to leave the stairs unattached so that they move when you're thrown into them. But the crew had put a steel bar through the stairs to hold them in place and then forgot to tell us. I went into the stairs like a linebacker and ricocheted off. It felt like hitting a brick wall. I thought I had broken my collarbone but pushed through the pain to the end of the match.

I think that might have started the herniation—I definitely didn't feel right after. Even though my collarbone was intact, I think I might have separated my shoulder and tweaked my upper back. But ultimately, it was my finisher, "The Rack Attack," that I realized was slowly breaking my neck. To do it, I lifted my opponent over my shoulders and then jumped to my knees—but this time it was like doing that while holding weights on my neck, and it was crunching me.

Over time my legs started to go numb. Every now and then I would walk and feel like they would be about to go out, or I'd wake up and they'd be completely numb. I told the doctors about it, and they told me to keep an eye on it but that it was probably nothing. I knew it was serious in Australia in July 2015, because my body kept giving out. My legs would just collapse out from beneath me during my finisher. I was sharing a room with Brie on that trip, and in the middle of the night I woke up because I couldn't lie down anymore. I stood in the bathroom for two hours crying because of the pain. I knew I was in trouble.

I had all these lumps all over my back and would lie on ice packs on the floor trying to get them to go down. I went to a naturopath who injected them with $CO_2$ gas, to see if he could get them to dissolve. I assumed that something was wrong with my back or my shoulder—I never thought that it could be my neck. I kept going to the doctor, but because my hands weren't numb, they told me that I was likely just tired and run-down because of the abuse I was putting my body through in the ring. I kept telling them that there was something wrong. I've been an athlete for my whole life and can distinguish wear and tear from injury.

I asked for an MRI, but they told me that it wouldn't show anything. They had no answer when I explained that my legs were going numb and giving out on me in matches, that I could only lie down in bed for a few hours at a time. Finally I had an MRI. I was in Austin, Texas, and I was backstage. A doctor came up to me to say: "Just so you know, we're not going to find anything." I would have given anything for that to be true.

I had dropped the title, and my rematch was coming up. I had a match in San Diego for *Raw* that I won, and then I flew to Phoenix for *SmackDown* the following night. I went for the MRI on that Tuesday afternoon before the taping. The doctor took one look at it and said: "This girl is about to break her neck in half." WWE sent me home. I wanted to see the WWE medical director but couldn't seem to get an appointment. Finally, I texted the office: "Is it because I'm a woman that I don't get the same treatment as the male Superstars?" I got an appointment. When he saw my MRI, his jaw dropped—he had only seen the same condition in one pro football player. He instructed me to get a cortisone epidural and rest to see if I could recover on my own without surgical intervention.

I went back to Tampa and went to the hospital to have the epidural. The ER doctor came in and told me that I was on the cusp of being paralyzed. It was clear that he didn't agree with my treatment plan. He told me to be incredibly careful—one slip, one fender bender, and it could be enough. I was really frustrated because I felt like if I were a male Superstar, I'd be getting radically different treatment instead of being instructed to just sit at home and pray.

That's when I asked Nattie to connect me with the neuro-surgeon who had worked on her husband, Tyson Kidd. He had suffered a career-ending neck fracture in 2015. Dr. Juan Uribe is one of the best neurosurgeons in the world, and he was willing to listen when I told him how lost and confused I felt. He asked for my MRI and then called me to tell me that I needed to see him immediately. He was shocked that I was even walking and couldn't believe that I hadn't had surgery.

With most neck injuries, the standard protocol is to go through the back and replace your neck with a fake one. But he told me that my life would essentially be ruined by that intervention, and that I could no longer be active in the same way. He felt like I was way too young. Dr. Uribe offered an alternative, though he cautioned me that it might not work. He suggested going in through the front of my neck. He created a special instrument, sort of like a candy cane, that he inserted into my neck to scrape off the herniation and then repair it like a bone fusion. He knew he wouldn't be able to get all of it out but thought he could get enough to make the surgery work. If it didn't work, he told me we'd have to resort to going through the back and doing a typical repair.

In January 2016, I underwent surgery and Dr. Uribe was successful. I had been told that my career was over, but I got back in the ring just seven months later. I managed to do it because I followed Dr. Uribe's instructions to a T. My family rallied around me to help me mend. Dr. Uribe instructed me to keep my brace on for six months straight, and for the first three months to not so much as get into a car—and if I had to get into a car, to stay off freeways. He told me that if I could commit to that, I'd come back strong. And he was absolutely right. I did my neck exercises and physical therapy, and I kept going to the gym, if only to lift two-pound hand weights and do some air squats. I knew I had to stay engaged and active if I wanted to wrestle again, that I couldn't let it all go by sitting on the couch in front of the TV.

When they took my brace off after six months, my neck wasn't fully fused, and likely it won't ever be. But I decided I wanted to stage my comeback seven months later, at *SummerSlam* in August, and I set my mind to it. I followed my physical therapy routine to a T, even though it felt at times like I was doing nothing and I would never get there, and I continued to do more as my doctor signed off.

I was working with my ex toward a massive match in April at *WrestleMania*. We were busy building story and momentum, but that final match very nearly didn't happen. A few weeks before *WrestleMania*, I messed up my timing and speared my head into Tyler Breeze's abs. When we collided, I felt this incredibly painful rush from my chin to the back of my skull. It felt like something was bursting out of my head. My head had even started bleeding. I had adrenaline though, so I managed to pick Tyler up and hit him with my Rack 2.0 finisher. My ex grabbed me, but I was in so much pain I couldn't even talk.

The doctors took me to the back, and I was so out of it they made the (correct) call that I couldn't wrestle that weekend. I went to see Dr. Uribe, who told me that I had herniated the disc above where I had the surgery. He felt strongly that I needed to be done with wrestling. This herniation would likely heal, but the minute I got another, I would need double bone fusion, or end up paralyzed or dead. I convinced him I would take it easy and not do a lot out there. I told him that I understood I could never be a full-time wrestler again.

This time around, WWE did not want to let me compete. I had to get X-rays and MRIs, and a litany of tests, to ensure that I would be okay. They didn't clear me until the Wednesday before my *WrestleMania* match. That match was meaningful to me for so many reasons. *WrestleMania* is a huge deal for women, in general, but this was my chance to do a match with my then current love. And as luck would have it, he then proposed to me in front of millions of WWE fans. It was a moment I had been waiting for my entire life.

As I promised to Dr. Uribe, I haven't been able to be a full-time wrestler since. I had to let that herniated disc heal, which took time (though it gave me an opportunity to do *Dancing with the Stars*). I'm very aware that if I get hit in the wrong way, that will be it for me in the same way that happened with Paige. Paige and I have a very similar injury. I never wanted to have to tell the women to be careful with me out there, but they all know they now have to avoid my neck at all costs. Even so, accidents happened. Best-laid plans and all of that.

It's a bummer, though. There are so many stories that I still want to tell in the ring. I wish I could have had a singles story with Sasha Banks, Asuka, Alexa Bliss, Bayley, and Becky Lynch. And I would love to finish my business with Charlotte Flair, who I was in a storyline with when my neck gave out. But I'm getting older now, and looking back at life in general, I've come to realize that health is first. There's so much more to life outside of wrestling. When I was younger, I wanted to die out there in the ring, but now I can recognize my wrestling career for what it's been—an incredible chapter of my life. Life-making, really. And I'm much more focused now on what I can do to help women outside of the ring, how I can continue to help women break barriers across industries. I'm excited to build brands with my sister that extend beyond the ring. I've become much more mature.

When you wrestle for as long as I have and have had as many major life moments in the ring, it's hard to find a moment of closure, when you can say, "I'm done," and feel good about it. I'm still waiting for the moment when I feel truly ready to hang up my snapback and Nikes, to acknowledge that it is okay that it is over, because I have had a helluva twelve-year-run. It's been particularly hard to find that moment because the sport for women has been rapidly changing recently, and I want to continue to see this movement through.

At first, I felt like closure would come at the *Royal Rumble* in January 2018, when the women got to do that historic match for the first time ever. Brie and I were thrilled when WWE asked us to be part of it. The *Royal Rumble* is a thirty-woman match that takes place over nearly an hour—and I almost fell over when they told me I would get to come out at #27 and work with the amazing Japanese wrestler Asuka. Vince is masterful at psychology, and so his thinking was that because Asuka is undefeated, the crowd would assume that Nikki Bella would be the one to break the streak. I had never wrestled her before, and it was incredible to work with her—she gave me a lot, and I don't think she'll ever know how grateful I am for that.

It was an incredible night with a not incredible finish. Asuka beat me and retained her winning streak, and then they made the decision to close it out by debuting Ronda Rousey. This was a little triggering for me in the moment. I unleashed a tweetstorm, which in retrospect was probably an overreaction. It was nothing against Ronda—it is thrilling that she is at WWE—but it was a bit of a slap in the face to all the historic women wrestlers who had come out for the match, the *main event*, only to have the moment upstaged by the Ronda announcement. It just didn't need to happen like that. It dominated the postshow news cycle and became the only thing everyone wanted to talk about—not the historic *Royal Rumble* and Asuka's dominance in the league. And by the way, it sucked for Ronda, too. Because that's no way to join a team—they threw her right into the lion's den.

As amazing as it was when we actually went live, the lead-up to the *Royal Rumble* was stressful. The men knew we were doing our finish, but that day they petitioned WWE to let them do that finish instead. And for some implausible reason, even though we were the main event, we were told that we would have to change our version. Asuka doesn't speak English, which made talking through variations hard. And we needed space to work, so they told us that we should drive back to the hotel (thirty minutes away) and work on something different in the ninety minutes before showtime. In a frantic dash, we worked up an alternative ending, and then the men changed their minds again and we were able to keep the original. It was one of the most stressful few hours of my life! Besides the unnecessary backflips, a bunch of guys were apparently pissed that we were the main event, too. We had waited decades for the historic opportunity; we deserved the chance to bask in it.

Moments and situations like those make me want to bang my head into the wall. Just give women one night! Let them do the finish they want to do without challenging it. Then don't debut a massive Superstar. It was a bummer because the women didn't get a chance to talk about what happened out there. We didn't get to tell the press that we'd had to abide by the same rules as the men, that we had to go over the top rope to be eliminated. Many of the girls out there had never gone over a top rope—it's scary! The interviews postshow would have been incredible. But instead, they'll never be able to capture the emotion of the event.

But that wasn't our last chance to change history. In the summer of 2018, Vince McMahon called to tell me that he was debuting *Evolution*, the first all-women pay-per-view event. And he asked me if I wanted to fight Ronda Rousey, the champion. While I thought I was done after the *Royal Rumble*, I jumped at the chance to come back and do a story with her in the ring.

In many ways, it was tough to stage a comeback. Physically, always, but it was particularly hard post-breakup with my fiancé. Everyone assumes that our *Total Bellas* TV storylines are fake, and that we put the drama on just like we do in the WWE ring. But the cameras capture everything, including the hard stuff. The show closely adheres to the reality of our lives. Throughout the comeback I was in a lot of pain. Besides the craziness of running two businesses and filming a reality show, I was crying myself to sleep every night and not sleeping. Those two-and-a-half months were some of my hardest yet. It didn't feel like the comeback that I wanted.

But the day of *Evolution*, it felt worth it—it was incredible. Backstage was full of emotion. It was such a strange experience to only see women, for one. And the energy from the crowd was coming all the way back to reach us. When I walked out on the ramp for the sold-out show, I realized that half of the audience was the Bella Army—they had turned up in spades. We had done a pep rally the night before, and they were supportive and amazing to all of us. I was hopeful that they would be ringside, but I had no idea what it would actually feel like to walk out and see an arena full of women and men holding Bella Army signs and screaming their heads off for all of us. That's a memory that will be seared into my mind for the rest of my life. Nothing can top that, even my main event match against Ronda. All the women that night left everything out there in the ring.

It finally felt like what we had been fighting for—for so long—had arrived. It was a movement for equality: being called by the same title, having the same time in the ring. It felt like respect and fairness. That night was career-justifying. That night was worth breaking my neck for.

# CHAPTER 8

# A STORY OF SUBMISSION

*2010-2018*

New York, New York

Las Vegas, Nevada

*Brie*

My now husband didn't tell me he loved me until the day he proposed. He had warned me in our early days of dating that he wouldn't say it. He had only ever told two people he loved them: his mom, Betty, and his sister, Billie Sue. He thought the way we all throw the word around—"I love this smoothie, I love the way these pants make my ass look, I love you, I love pasta"—cheapened it, made it meaningless. I thought it was a funny thing to say at the time. It was so very Bryan, who loves making rules and then actually sticking to them. I didn't think it was a big deal, because I honestly didn't think we'd ever be serious enough to say it.

I first met Bryan in February 2010. He'd had an epic and long career in the independents—and was an internet darling thanks to his high-flying, technical Japanese wrestling style. For context, he has had several documented concussions in his career, and he started racking them up early on. His first came in Japan, when he went to do a backflip off the top rope onto the floor. In WWE, the top rope is made of rope, but in Japan it's a cable covered in a PVC-like plastic. Bryan's feet rolled and he crashed headfirst into the floor. The second came in Austin, Texas, in 2000, when he did a front flip off the top rope and his opponent failed to catch him. The third, only a week later, was when he planned to jump off the top rope and through a table, but he overshot the other guy and cracked his head on the metal spoke in the table after he went through it. To put it lightly, he is one of those guys who fully paid his dues working up the ranks. He would tell you that he didn't know if he even wanted a career in WWE, which is more performative and less risky, from a wrestling perspective, than the indies. But the money is certainly better.

Before we were ever in a storyline together, we talked for the first time at the baggage claim in New York City. I had just moved to the city, and it was clear that he had no clue which Bella I was—he distinguished the two of us as the one who lived in New York City and the one who lived in San Diego. A few months later, they developed a storyline for me and Nicole where we were both in hot pursuit of him (he picked his WWE Superstar name, Daniel Bryan, by the way, over Buddy Peacock . . . even though Buddy Peacock would definitely be a great porn name) because we had heard that his virginity was up for grabs. The punchline was that he wasn't a virgin—he was actually a *vegan*. At first Bryan hated the concept since he thought it made him look like a loser. He wasn't used to the campiness of WWE at that point—or how you can work silly storylines to become a fan favorite—but he warmed up to the story over time. The funniest "oops," which he recounted in his own memoir, was when we were working an entrance where he'd squat and we'd step on his thighs to get up into the ring—in that moment, during a live event, we realized we had both forgotten to put on underwear. I wish I could say this was a one-off, but we frequently forgot our underwear, and we probably gave everyone ringside an accidental show. He also convinced us to join in on this airplane gimmick—we would make plane arms as we would valet him down the ramp. Then he would pick up Teddy DiBiase Jr. and airplane him over his head until Teddy was really dizzy. Then Nicole would pick up Maryse, Teddy's valet, and spin her around until she was really dizzy. Then I would slap Maryse, and Maryse would slap Teddy, and then roll him up for her finisher until he'd kick out. Then Bryan would roll him up and put his finisher on him. It was good, dorky WWE fun.

Romantically, I had never cared much about the WWE guys. I was friends with a bunch of them but preferred to hang out with bartenders and handsome strangers in New York City, rather than sleep where I worked. And Bryan really wasn't my type—I had always gone for tatted-up artsy skaters and musicians, not mountain men from Aberdeen, Washington, who came from a long lineage of loggers. But we were working together, and so we would chat before and after matches, and we found that we had a lot in common. I have always been an environmentalist, even though I didn't really know at the time how to articulate what that meant. I had always just felt a kinship with nature, an aversion to industrialization, a desire to preserve and not waste (even when I was a kid, I would reuse paper to send letters to my sister, writing over old notes). Bryan was also, if more ardently, committed to saving the earth. We had both thought about joining the Peace Corps. It's weird to find those types of synergies within the ranks of WWE, which isn't exactly known as being a bedrock of bohemianism.

One night when I was driving to the next town with Nicole, I told her that maybe I was developing some feelings for Bryan. I went on to explain how much we had in common, even though he was nothing like the other guys I had dated. We believed in the same things. Her response was classic Nicole: "That's really weird." I thought it was pretty weird, too, and I really didn't want a boyfriend. I was just out of half a decade with Craig and was craving independence and freedom. But we were on the same show and live events together, and I was finding myself becoming more and more drawn to him.

We typically didn't have to be at the arena until late—around 5 p.m., unless it was a TV event, in which case we needed to be there a few hours earlier. I usually tried to hit up a museum or cultural event in whatever city we happened to be visiting. When we stopped in Boston for that year's *Royal Rumble*, I texted Bryan to see if he wanted to go to the Isabella Stewart Gardner museum with me. I had been dying to go. During her life, Gardner amassed a stunning collection, including Renaissance masterpieces. Then she built them a Venetian palace–inspired home at the turn of the twentieth century, making it unlike most museums. Bryan told me he'd love to go, and we jumped in his car.

I was crushing on Bryan as we wandered the floors of this quiet and idyllic museum. I don't get embarrassed easily, but early on, I pointed to a painting—I guess I was close to it—and a security guard started yelling at me:

"Hey, don't point at the painting!" I wanted to snap back, "You can't yell at me in front of a guy I have a crush on!" It was humiliating. Bryan and I were both giddy and charged in that way you are when you're curious about where something could go (and maybe waiting to be kissed, which never came that day). We kept wandering, looking at art, and talking until we realized that we were going to be late for the show and bolted—Bryan in a total panic because he has an aversion to being late (I wish I had that). On the drive back to the arena, I had to reassure him that they wouldn't fire him or kick his ass for being five minutes late. To this day, we still haven't made it back to see the third floor of that museum.

I'll never forget the early days in our storyline, when, for example, the three of us were sent to a Verizon Wireless store outside of Washington, D.C., for an appearance. None of us were particularly well known at that point, and WWE hadn't done a lot to promote it. We just sat in this Verizon Wireless, waiting to sign for fans who did not come. It could not have been more random or hilarious. Three professional wrestlers, posted up between the cell phones and the cases. That's when Bryan told me that neither of us should reproduce—in general; he wasn't even talking about him and me together. He believes that we've stopped evolving because of modern medicine, and that the lives of many people have been saved who weren't supposed to survive. He was a very sick child, with bad allergies, viral asthma, and a weak immune system. Meanwhile, I should have died in the womb or shortly thereafter, because my mom didn't realize she was pregnant with twins and stopped pushing after Nicole came out, leaving me in there without oxygen for a dangerous amount of time. At that point, I actually had a crush on the guy. I just remember thinking: "What the hell are you talking about, you weirdo?" Where was the romance?

Our storyline was coming to an end. In our competition for his virginity, Nikki and I had both kissed him, but popping his cherry wasn't exactly going to work on TV. In a backstage promo, we walked in on him with another Diva, Gail Kim, who he told us was his girlfriend. "But we thought you were a . . ." He jumped in: "Vegan? Absolutely, I don't eat any meat." We went on to fight Gail and I got to hit Bryan in the face (or ear, to hear him recount it). That culminating scene was fun, but it meant that I no longer had any reason to hang out with Bryan. That made me sad, which then forced the realization that I might have more than a crush on him. Our storyline ended on a Monday, which was remarkable only because it was also February 14.

The next day, we were in San Diego for *SmackDown Live*. I went with a bunch of friends, Nicole, and another wrestler she was dating to Nick's at the Beach after the show. And I invited

Bryan. He came back to Nicole's condo with us. I think he was weirded out because he didn't realize that Nicole and Brad were seeing each other, though that was more due to the fact that he never really paid attention to that sort of stuff than the fact that it was a secret. We all hung out for a while. It was getting late, and so I walked him back to his car, which was parked a few blocks away. Nothing happened, but he offered to drive me back to Nicole's. We obviously knew we liked each other at this point. It was after Boston and a few other couples' excursions—and yet we just sat parked outside of Nicole's, like two awkward teenagers. I thought to myself: "Is he actually waiting for *me* to make the first move?" Then I opened the door with an "Okay, bye!" and bolted upstairs. In Bryan's version of events, I essentially jumped out of the car while it was still moving, though he acknowledges that it was a good five seconds. Count it out, that's a long time to sit there and wait for a kiss!

I went back upstairs, a little annoyed and disheartened. I stopped to chat with Nicole and Brad about why Bryan was being such a dolt about making a move. Nicole offered me pretty basic advice: "Text him to come back and kiss you." So I went up to Nicole's spare room, and sprawled out in bed in my pajamas, and wrote: "I thought you were a gentleman and were going to kiss me good night." He replied that I shouldn't tempt him, and that he was turning his car around. I got out of bed, and promptly tripped over the comforter. Nicole came to see why it sounded like I had been tackled, and I told her about Bryan's U-turn. It was so awkward.

I probably should have brushed my teeth. The elevator in her building was unreliable, and so I took the stairs. I felt like I was doing a reverse walk of shame. Bryan was down there waiting for me, and as I went to open the gate, he grabbed me and gave me a kiss. It's funny, because I thought he was going to be a bad kisser—maybe I had bounced from the car because I had been scared to find out—but he was fantastic. That's high praise coming from a kissing bandit like me.

We stood outside and made out for a while. Bryan thinks it was raining, but I don't remember that—and then that was it. A perfectly PG-13 romantic moment. I ran back upstairs to Nicole's, and he headed back to his hotel before flying home to Las Vegas. To this day, we still mark February 15 as our anniversary.

After that, Bryan and I started to date. We kept the fact that we were seeing each other a secret at work. Nicole and her boyfriend were really the only ones who knew. At that time, when relationships were open at WWE there was always a lot of stigma. Other wrestlers would put a lot of negativity around it—plotting and wishing for its demise, seeding shit. We're a dramatic crew! I'm not sure what that was about, but it was definitely a thing back then (now everyone seems to be in a relationship with another wrestler). There was also always the threat, which I don't think was ever real, that the top creative brass at WWE would separate you and put you on two different franchises. I'm sure there was some truth to all of this, but there was also a lot of myth-making. Regardless, Bryan and I vowed to keep it just between us for as long as we could.

It *almost* all came out at the end of February in Fresno. I had picked Bryan up from the arena, and we went back to the hotel—I think it was a Holiday Inn Express—to get it on, for the first time ever. Bryan is really romantic, and "quickie" is not part of his vocabulary. He loves to set a mood, take his time, light some candles, bust out the massage oil. Bryan's travel buddies, Sheamus and Teddy DiBiase Jr., saw me picking up Bryan after he had shrugged off joining them for dinner. They openly pointed and laughed at us before heading their own way. What we didn't realize was that they were actually booking it back to the hotel. All the guys had checked in at the same time earlier, and so the front desk attendant didn't ask for ID and gave them a copy of Bryan's room key. A few minutes later they busted in on us—before anything had officially happened, though neither of us had any clothes on. Bryan charged them, buck naked, and tried to kick Teddy in the head; I had crawled under the pillows and Sheamus just sat there and patted me on the head. It was, in retrospect, a story for the ages. It still makes us laugh—but Bryan was so flipped out that we ended up skipping sex and just going straight to bed. It was, in short, a mood killer.

For months, I would travel to the next town with Nicole, and then sneak into Bryan's hotel room at night. Ultimately, we spent about five nights of the week together when we were on the road for WWE. Then we would separate for a couple of days so I could head to New York and he could go home to Las Vegas, where he was living at the time. Those were great days. Nicole and I would arrive very late at night—typically between 2 and

3 a.m., depending on the length of the drive. Then Bryan and I could spend the entire next day hanging out in bed, with a brief break for a workout. It's a strange schedule, but it's perfect for that beginning-of-relationship stuff when you just want to cuddle, chat, and watch bad TV.

It was really not my intent to date a wrestler, primarily because when you inevitably break up, you still have to see each other at work all week and then you'll likely see them with the next wrestler they happen to get involved with. But a relationship of some sort with Bryan just seemed inevitable. As much as I didn't intend for it to happen in the first place, there was no way to stop it once it started. Except, of course, by refusing to be his girlfriend.

Once we started having sex, he jumped to the natural conclusion that we were boyfriend/girlfriend, whereas I thought we were just having casual sex. When I was back in New York City, it's not like I wanted to go out and get action—but I did want to revel in my freedom along with my girlfriends. And officially, I had been seeing someone in New York who I needed to shake off. He was an Italian guy who owned a wine company. For me, he epitomized living in the city, having freedom, having a good time, having a relationship without pressure and labels. I knew he wasn't the one, which only made it more fun. Ultimately, I had to end things with him. Maybe he could sense that there was someone else in the picture, but he began to want more from me, and I was falling for Bryan. After it ended with the Italian, it was weird. While I maintained that I was in an open relationship with Bryan and absolutely free to date other people, I didn't meet anyone else. Nobody really grabbed my attention because Bryan really did have it all. I just didn't want to admit it to myself.

Bryan hated New York. While the city made me feel alive, independent, and like a woman, it made him feel overwhelmed and miserable. On the flip side, I hated going to Las Vegas with a fierce passion. While I would never officially kick a relationship to the curb because of location and real estate, from the outset I assumed our relationship was doomed. In my mind I had sworn forever allegiance to Manhattan. I thought, like Carrie Bradshaw, it might be my one true love.

A few months in, when we were sitting in bed together in Europe in April 2011, Bryan formally asked me to be his girlfriend. And I said no. And then he asked me again a few weeks later, and I said no again. Finally, after asking me yet again, he told me that if I didn't commit, he was done. He gave me an ultimatum. I couldn't bring myself to cave, simply because I didn't want to be a girlfriend. It seemed really important to me at the time and not giving in was a doubling down on that. I didn't want a serious relationship. I just wanted freedom, which included the freedom to see as much of him as I wanted.

It all came to a head because Bryan is a teetotaler—because of his dad's history with alcohol he just won't touch the stuff. I, on the other hand, love my wine. I love to get into Brie Mode when it's merited, when I just . . . have the time of my life. I'm a happy drunk. I'm good to have at a party. We were together, wrestling in the lead-up to New Year's Eve on the East Coast, and then we had a short, one-day break before we needed to be in Memphis. Bryan asked me about my New Year's plans and I shrugged him off. In retrospect, not the right thing to do. When you care about someone, you should usher in the New Year together. But I wanted to Brie Mode it out without Bryan's judgment, and I thought his dislike for New York City would put a damper on the night. Plus, our contract was coming up and it seemed likely that Nicole and I would walk away from WWE. So I think I had started to subtly push him away.

The next day, he broke up with me on the phone. My sister was staying with me at the time. I walked home to my apartment in Greenwich Village, and then I started to bawl. I told her that my heart hurt, and that I was really sad—I didn't want to lose him. Nicole, ever the relationship savant, pointed out that maybe if I didn't want to lose him, I should not give him away. Then Bryan called and said: "I'd rather have half of you, than none of you." And I replied, "I would rather have all of you, than none of you."

Later that day, I went to Washington Square Park and sat in the sun and wrote a pros and cons list about Bryan. The "pros" came easily, whereas I had to dig deep for the "cons." Everything I came up with to fill that column seemed really stupid and trivial: "Doesn't like New York. Doesn't drink. Is a wrestler." As I sat there in the cold winter sun and thought about Bryan, something in my heart felt warm and satisfied. I flew to Las Vegas to see him and make it official. We were sitting in his room, for which he paid $700 a month, listening to Pearl Jam. I asked him to be my boyfriend. He said no.

"It doesn't feel good, does it?" he asked.

Then he said, "Yes."

About three weeks later, I had a call to check in with a medium whom I speak to pretty regularly. While Bear sends me signs constantly, I still like to have a direct line to hear confirmation and validation that he can hear me. She asked me if I had been in a park recently thinking about Bryan, and I confirmed that in fact I had been. "Bear wants you to know that he was shining so much light and sunshine on you, that you made the right decision, that the glow you felt in your heart was real." This wasn't the first time that I felt like Bear had sent Bryan to me, but it did feel like the first official confirmation that Bryan was the right choice. While I wasn't calling her to justify my decision—I had already made up my mind—it was nice to know that Bear approved nonetheless.

As Bryan and I became more and more involved, our relationship became impossible to hide. We finally outed ourselves at *WrestleMania XVII* in Atlanta. We were just always together, and people catch on when there's a certain amount of intimacy. The only alternative was to avoid each other entirely, and that wasn't appealing. Plus, it felt real enough that it was worth being open about it backstage. As a bonus, Bryan was able to start driving from city to city with me and Nicole, which broke up some of the time behind the wheel. I don't think it's just a twin thing, but there's something really special about watching two people you love come to love each other, too.

We were like *Three's Company*. Bickering, laughing, and teasing. Nicole and Bryan's relationship is based on giving each other shit—we would call her Third Wheel Nikki. They have seemingly different values, and so there is endless territory where they completely disagree. Plus, Nicole and I have a pretty limited vocabulary, whereas Bryan is the king of big, smart words. That alone was pure comedy—it's where the idea for "Bella Brains," our YouTube quiz show, came from. These jokes made the miles pass quickly, even though Bryan is the slowest driver. The funniest moment had to be when he was pulled over for speeding on our way to Yakima, Washington, which felt like a total impossibility—Bryan drives under the speed limit, never even 5 mph over. But he had picked up some speed accidentally coming down a hill and got slapped with a ticket. Nicole and I howled with laughter. We made local food our big thing, and would always hunt down the town's culinary gems, like pancake balls in Columbus, Ohio. On Tuesday mornings, Nicole and Bryan would go work out together while I slept in. I really love to sleep in.

Bryan also learned that just because I love nature doesn't mean that I'm not scared of it. In the early days, I really had to pee as we were driving through the backwoods of Mississippi. Bryan kept offering to pull over, but I was too scared to go to the bathroom in the grass because of the bugs. So he pulled into a gas station and I peed . . . in the parking lot. Understandably, he thought it was really weird. It *was* weird. But man, I hate bugs.

Bryan is really thoughtful. The Valentine's Day after we started dating, he sent Nicole a gorgeous bouquet of roses with the note:

"Because every woman deserves flowers on Valentine's Day."
Meanwhile, he had sent me a vegan cupcake from the Red Velvet
Café in Las Vegas that arrived smashed. It turns out he had sent
me roses, too, but they got held up and arrived later that night. It
was pretty hilarious to have spent all day dissecting his intent.

Ultimately, I gave up New York for my relationship with
Bryan. We toyed with the idea of finding a bigger apartment there
in Dumbo or the Financial District, but Bryan just didn't think
he would be happy in a city where the natural world plays such
a small role. I could understand that. Living apart wasn't enough
of a reason for me to keep holding on to my studio in Greenwich
Village, but Vegas was a nonstarter for me, too. We ended up
moving to San Diego, where we could at the very least be closer
to my family.

Bryan and I moved in together in May 2012, just weeks after
Nicole and I ended up leaving WWE. We were too frustrated to
stay—with the lack of equality, the lack of good storylines, the
short matches. So we left, even though it meant that I would
spend a majority of most weeks away from my boyfriend. While
WWE asked for us back (we returned about eleven months later,
with our *Total Divas* TV show), I wasn't having the same luck
bringing Bryan to submission around the whole "I love you" conversation. When you're in love, it's really hard to not say it all the
time. I'm expressive, I'm unfiltered, I'm used to saying exactly
what I think. But Bryan, just as he had declared at the very beginning, wouldn't cough it up. I used to sing Skidamarink a-dink, a
dink on repeat ("Skidamarink a-dink, a-dink, Skidamarink a-doo,

I love you"), leaving out the "I love you's" for him to fill in. When I passed the torch to him to fill in the blanks, he would just stick out his tongue.

On September 25, 2013, on a hike in Big Sur, California, Bryan dropped to one knee and asked me to marry him. Perhaps more important, he told me he loved me. It's funny, because even though it was irritating to have to wait—and I definitely had moments of wondering how I had managed to get involved with a man who couldn't stomach three simple words—I got what he meant about love becoming a little cheap with overuse. When he finally said it, it was incredible, even though I knew he had loved me for a long time. He always made me feel cherished. He said it with his eyes, his actions, the way he looked at me, touched me, protected me, and nurtured me. On the flip side, I've been with many guys who said "I love you" all day long, but never made me feel like there was any intention behind their words. (Speaking of teaching each other how to say things, I have certainly expanded Bryan's vocabulary, as he now regularly uses chick language like "So good," and "amazing," which he thinks are imprecise and hyperbolic.)

We had had a couple of epic fights about the L-word over the course of our relationship—not so much about his refusal, but about the fact that he can be so rigid and unyielding. And about the fact that he has so many rules, whereas I'm a free spirit. With Bryan, it was a lot of "I don't drink, I don't say 'I love you,' I don't . . . ," which led me to the inevitable question: "Then what do you do?" I'll spare you all the details, but there was one moment when we were dating where we didn't use protection even though we *always* did, and I checked in with him after.

"Are you sure you're okay? You always said after marriage, and I know you have rules about this."

"It's fine."

"Are you sure?"

"It's fine."

When we were done, he told me that he needed to go take a shower "and think about this." Now, obviously, that made me feel really bad. I wanted to be cuddled, not feel like I had defiled him. After, when he came back into the room, he said: "I'm fine with the decision." I'll never forget his exact phrasing. What a wonderful weirdo.

Bryan's proposal was on camera, though he was so nervous he forgot to say most of what he had planned. He made peanut butter and jelly sandwiches, and we sat on a cliff overlooking the ocean while he told me twenty things he loved about me. I guess I had told him that I didn't care where he proposed or when, but that the words were really important. That's a lot of pressure! Of course, neither of us actually remember what came out of his mouth. He also told me that he had wanted to propose on the third floor of the Isabella Stewart Gardner Museum, but this sweeping view of the ocean (which he likened to our love) would have to do. We were staying at "The Jewel in the Forest," which is essentially a dome in the woods for hippies like us. It was the first time we ever went to the bathroom in front of each other because the toilet faced the bed—there might have been a few strings of beads for privacy. Bryan got to hear me poop while he looked me in the eyes. I loved that we reached a whole new level of intimacy at a moment when we had decided to cement our relationship. I was fine with the decision.

We got married in a rush, in part because they really wanted it for *Total Divas*. Since our relationship had been documented there, we thought it seemed fair. Plus, Bryan is a pushover. If we had to do it over, I think we would have tried to stretch it out, so it wasn't all a blur. Bryan had his title match in *WrestleMania 30*—a massive, massive moment in his career. Then we were married the following Friday. We also closed on our first house. It was a lot, probably too much. But it's also hard to want anything to be different when it was amazing despite the condensed timeline.

Maybe it's that Nicole and I were raised in a farming family, and were always around animals, but I've always felt most comfortable in nature—and I've always had a deep kinship with Native American cultures. When genetic testing came along, I wasn't surprised to discover that we're actually part Native American. I grew up with a lot of love and respect for the land, and always found places like the more industrial parts of New Jersey to be really disturbing—like the land was being pillaged and denuded in a way that didn't seem just or sustainable. But Bryan is a next-level environmentalist. Give the guy a composting toilet, a gray water system, and the opportunity to live off the grid, and he's really happy. If I wouldn't vehemently object, he'd build an outhouse in our backyard, hook up a rain shower, and turn off our water.

Bryan and I are both vegetarians, which hasn't been a lifelong choice for me. I had tried it in my twenties—then pescetarian, ultimately—but now it's how we live, and it feels right to me. In theory I'd love to become vegan, but I'm not quite ready to give up on the cheese plate. When Bryan goes on the road, I pretty much live on wine, pickles, and cheese—and not the kind made from cashews. Bryan has taught me a lot about sustainability over the years, and really pushed me to be better at what I believe in. I love our environmentally friendly life and take a lot of pride in the fact that we're good role models and protectors of the earth. And the added pressure of all those eyes on us has probably made us double down on it, too.

It's funny, because in contrast Nicole seems like she's consumed with superficial things. But that's selling her short, because she absolutely gets it. In fact, she has lost out on tons of money because of me. We've turned down a lot of deals from big fast-food companies simply because I couldn't get comfortable with their factory farming practices. She never tries to strong-arm me into doing it (though we did toy around with the idea that I could donate my share to the ASPCA or Sierra Club in a subtle middle finger). Instead she vows that she will never make me do something that goes against my beliefs. Bryan always calls Nicole when he needs gift advice for me, which I'm sure boils down to her advising him to go and buy me some shoes made out of recycled tires, or a purse made from trash bags. She doesn't try to foist the stuff that she likes on me. Even though she lives a five-star life, she's sacrificed a lot for me and she never complains; she's always known who I am.

I grew up lower middle-class, but Bryan grew up really poor. He lives in constant fear of never having enough, even though we have plenty. We live as small as possible—both to limit our environmental footprint and also because enough is just perfectly enough. My only goal in life is to have a savings account that will cover us in case of emergencies so I don't have to wake up in the middle of the night stressed about making our mortgage. And if I can, I love to fly business class. I've been spoiled a bit in the last couple of years, though I spent a decade flying across the country for WWE in the back of the plane. It's one big splurge that Bryan and I agree on. (This is not to say that I don't still sometimes fly coach, which I just did the other week with Birdie on my lap—we sat in the bitch seat, in the back of the plane, in the row of seats in front of the bathrooms.)

Right now, we have two homes. My husband will not give up on Washington State, and when I had Birdie, I felt acutely that I needed to be close to family in San Diego, and I needed sun. We made a compromise and built a house in Port Townsend, which is a cute town outside of Seattle. It's in the rain shadow, meaning it's not quite as wet. Then we found something to rent in California. I did finally convince him that we needed to give up his childhood home in Aberdeen. His mom was making more use of it than we were, and it still seemed like it belonged to her. And probably rightfully so. I didn't feel comfortable dismantling it in order to make it my own, since it clearly held a huge amount of sentimental value for him. He said I could change it, but I never felt like I could do anything other than add a throw pillow or two. After all, if Bryan wanted to preserve something from childhood, then he should keep it preserved. I'm not sure why houses have never really meant anything to me—I think it's because my own home growing up was never a fun place to be, so I never grew attached.

I envy people who have one home, with their family nearby in the same town. It's hard because Bryan's sister lives in Pennsylvania, my mom is in Tampa, my dad is in Mexico, my brother is in Phoenix, my sister is everywhere. What I wouldn't give to not have to travel over the holidays but just root down with everyone, all in the same place. So it will be in our next lives.

Besides Aberdeen, the only other thing we've really fought about in our relationship is booze. Bryan's dad was an alcoholic, which was debilitating for both him and the family. He walked out when Bryan was young, leaving Bryan's mom to struggle to make ends meet as a single mom. Bryan did maintain a relationship with him during the times he was able to stay sober. Bryan is rigid and rule-based, and at a very young age he vowed to never even test his tendency for alcoholism. He has never had a sip of alcohol, he's never tried a drug, he's never had a drag of a cigarette. But he does have the addiction gene: He has designated days to eat sweets because if left to his own devices, he'll stand over the sink and smash ten cupcakes in under ten minutes. Sugar is his drug.

I on the other hand have trouble wrapping up a day without a glass of wine. Besides being the signal to myself that it's time to unwind, it's the primary way that I socialize. I love to have a drink while watching the sunset, I love happy hour with friends, and when the occasion demands it, I love to get into full-on Brie Mode. When we were courting each other, it was tough to not be able to fall back on a typical drinks-at-the-bar fail-safe date.

While the idea of Bryan being able to enjoy a drink with me is tempting, I'm relieved that he is so unrelenting about not even trying it. It was just frustrating at various points of our relationship when he expected me to be the same. In the early days, he treated me like a burgeoning alcoholic. He used to be so judgmental—when I'd go to order a second drink, he'd stare at me from across the table. "Don't go old big bug eyes on me!" I'd yell. I wouldn't back down or let him cow me into limiting my drinking, because I know I don't have a problem with booze. I knew that if I were to give in to his pressure, it'd be over. I refuse to be policed by my husband—to me, that doesn't sound like a relationship, that sounds like jail. I've always been the loud party girl. Nicole and I were the ones on the bus during the WWE European tours singing and drinking wine and DJ-ing with Santino. Bryan thought we were "those really annoying Bella twins," but it was fun, and those trips were always the most bonding. Nowadays, people are more inclined to dive into their iPads. But at that time, those bus trips were the best. Bryan has always known that that's how I like to roll. I'm the type of girl who likes to get drunk and do interpretive dances.

Ultimately, I had to have a big talk with him and remind him that I'm not his father. If I don't feel like having a drink, I can certainly abstain. I'm perfectly capable of having a dry January or cooling it when I feel like I've had enough. When I was pregnant with Birdie, he asked me not to drink even a sip of alcohol. I felt like I had to give that to him, even though most women I know felt like they couldn't get through the third trimester without an occasional glass of wine. Near the end, when she wouldn't come and I was going days past my due date, my acupuncturist directed me to go home and have a glass of wine. But no dice.

The addict gene isn't the only one Bryan has to contend with. There's also a pretty terrible history of depression on his dad's side of the family, and Bryan has struggled with it through-out his life. I definitely think that the concussions he's suffered have amplified this tendency. Though to hear him tell it, he's always been Eeyore. He has struggled with crippling bouts of depression since he was a kid. He can feel them coming, and just puts himself to bed until they pass. He understands all the while that it is a chemical imbalance and not a deeper statement about who he is; he has also learned ways of minimizing the attacks, typically through watching what he eats and exercising every morning.

I think the other reason I'm dedicated to living well within our means is that I don't want the added pressure of being per-formers for the rest of our lives—particularly because it's not necessarily possible. When Bryan was forced to retire in 2016 because of issues from concussions, he was devastated. He'd known he couldn't wrestle forever and was prepared to leave at some point—but he wanted it to be on his own terms, not on doctor's orders.

Because of this, he suffered from a mental breakdown, compounded by debilitating depression. It was horrible to watch, and as Bryan's wife and partner, it was scary, too. When you're defined by one thing for decades, and it's no longer yours to own, you can lose your entire sense of self. Bryan went back to WWE to be a general manager, in the hopes that being around wrestling would be satisfying enough. But he always felt like going back without being able to get in the ring actually impeded him from getting over it and finding something else to do with his life. He had to watch from the sidelines as his friends wrestled, when he wanted so much to join them.

When forced into retirement, Bryan spent an insane amount of energy getting cleared to return to the ring. He traveled across the United States meeting with doctors—all of whom believed that he was well enough to wrestle, his brain was not irretrievably damaged, and his neck was sturdy enough (he broke it in 2014, on live TV). But ultimately it was up to WWE. I have always told Bryan that I will support him in whatever he wants to do. I'll never hold him back, because I know that I would resist being held back myself. I firmly believe that nobody should have dominion over someone. We're all here to live our own lives.

*That said*, Bryan knows what could happen if he causes irretrievable brain damage through one more bad fall. It's just not worth it if any of the doctors think it's a risk he shouldn't take. I think trying something new could be amazing for Bryan—he's a brilliant guy, passionate about the earth and the environment, intent on leaving it in a better place than when he found it. I would love to see him working outdoors, expressing his love for animals and the planet, putting his energy into something like watershed management or telling the world why everyone needs a composting toilet.

But he's not done wrestling. In March 2018, he landed in Texas from Saudi Arabia and had a voicemail from Dr. Maroon that he wanted to see him. He boarded the next flight to Pittsburgh, ran through a handful of tests, and then Dr. Maroon slipped a piece of paper across the desk that said, "Finally, you're cleared!" He was immediately on a flight to Texas for *Smack-Down*, where he was power bombed by Kevin Owens. I watched him on TV that night and could see him fighting back a massive smile—only Bryan would welcome a power bomb from a 266-pound man.

I think that Bryan's story is really inspirational. I feel that he needs to spend some time out on the road speaking, letting people know that they're not alone if they suffer from depression or mental illness. We filmed his complete breakdown for *Total Bellas*—it was all on tape. He had the option to cut it, but we ended up airing a significant portion of it. He wanted other people who are feeling the same way, who grapple with the same types of issues, to see him tackle it head-on. He wanted the world to know that it's okay to be depressed, it's okay to be devastated when something that you love is taken away from you. You can grow from it and ultimately thrive. You can find a way to reconcile yourself to depression's presence in your life without letting it paralyze you from going after what you want.

People who are depressed don't want to be alone. They want to find a path to achieving their dreams alongside people who love them, too.

When we got married, Bryan reminded me that his depression is his biggest flaw. I might argue that it's a strength, as I believe that it has stretched him as a man and made him even more compassionate and wonderful than he might otherwise have been. I reminded him that I am a pistol and that that's probably *my* biggest flaw. I am very easy to trigger, as my parents never modeled fighting with your partner in a way that didn't go dark and malicious. I have had to do a lot of "re-parenting" to find new ways to funnel my anger in a more productive way. Fighting with your spouse is normal, but Bryan would argue that I don't know how to fight well, or in a way where it's easy to walk it back from the brink.

One time I called Bryan a "total fucking idiot" in public—in Sea-Tac Airport to be exact—and he didn't speak to me for two days. And to be honest, I've called him something *like* a fucking idiot more than once. Now that's mean, kind of unconscionably mean, and obviously not true. But I didn't have the self-regulation to express my displeasure in a less intense and angry way. I would just flare up, express, and then be forced to repent in a pretty significant way.

Here's how it started. We were eating breakfast at Anthony's in the Seattle airport. We were heading to San Diego so Bryan could meet my grandma. He went to the bathroom—and left all his stuff at the table with me, including his phone, wallet, etc.—

and then he didn't come back. I figured he was having some issues and so waited for a bit before I realized that our flight was
boarding. I packed up all his stuff, grabbed my bags, his bags,
and dragged it all to the bathroom. I asked a random guy to go
in there and look for the bearded mountain man, and he told me
he wasn't in there. Then they called final boarding and I had to
sprint—with all of our stuff—to the gate, where I found Bryan
just standing there.

He claims that he went back to Anthony's and I wasn't there.
I had somehow vanished myself or decided to pull a prank and
asked a busboy to hide me and our luggage. I obviously hadn't
moved. I was pissed, particularly because he kept maintaining
that I wasn't there. (The restaurant had two entrances, so he
had clearly gone into the wrong one.) We started arguing as we
boarded and then I threw his shit—in front of everyone—and
called him a fucking idiot.

He pretty much treated me like I was the worst person in
the world throughout the weekend. He couldn't have been nicer
to my grandmother (otherwise we wouldn't be married), but he
didn't speak to me for days. Finally, we addressed it and got down
deep with it. He told me that in his family, they didn't talk to each
other like that. He was literally rendered speechless by what I
could send out of my mouth. I explained that in my family, we
did. (Nicole and I are notorious for ripping each other's throat out,
cussing each other out, and then going to grab coffee together
a few minutes later like nothing happened.) From that day on,
whenever I said anything mean, he wrote it down in a journal. It

was actually a good way for him to give me visible proof of some pretty bad behavior that came in the heat of the moment, when I was almost unconscious with rage. He's also come to realize that meeting my pain with coldness isn't a way to move us forward either. It has been a slow but worthwhile process, one filled with labor and love.

# CHAPTER 9

# RACK ATTACK

*2012-2019*

Land O' Lakes, Florida

San Diego, California

*Nicole*

My first date with my ex was at Gibsons Steakhouse in Chicago, and the rest is *Total Divas* and *Total Bellas* rerun history. For the purpose of his privacy, I don't want to retread old events here—particularly the ones that got plenty of screen time and rehashing in the media. There is not much more to milk from that well-documented chain of events. But I do think there is value in explaining what I learned about myself during a time of extreme highs and lows, in the hopes that it helps some of you.

I have many regrets about that relationship. The primary one is that I wish I'd known myself better before I got into it. I wish

I'd understood how the patterns in my life, and my relationship with my own father, informed how I react to love, boundaries, and feelings of abandonment. I think I could have averted some of what happened. Because my dad left when I was fifteen, I learned how to fill in the holes. I expect to be left behind and to find a way to not confront or acknowledge those feelings of loneliness and abandonment. It's almost scarier to me when someone seems like they're sticking around. I've learned that it puts me in a position of expecting the worst, waiting for the other shoe to drop. I believe that it actually causes me to panic.

Because I am a chin-up type of girl, I feed myself a diet of deprivation. I assume that I don't need anyone to help me survive and thrive—and I think this mind-set meant I never processed my feelings. I've just always been focused on moving forward, step by step; on getting up every time I'm knocked to the ground. While my ex and I tried our hardest not to go too long without seeing each other, looking back, I don't think it was enough. It is easy to recognize that our long stints on the road and working all of our various side hustle jobs left me feeling almost pathologically lonely. I just didn't know how to identify the emotion. And I certainly didn't know how to ask for what I needed. I was intent on fitting into the contours of my ex's very busy and big life. That was paramount to me, pleasing and keeping him content, not voicing my own needs. He had no idea I wasn't getting what I needed because I never said anything.

The "pleasing" bug is another side effect from my turbulent childhood. I am attached to a very disturbing core belief that I am only lovable when I put other people first. That I only deserve their affection because I am useful and handy. I learned from my ex that this is a profound fallacy. He could see the real me and love me just the same. It felt too good to be true; I felt undeserving.

We also struggled to align on what we both wanted, because from the outset we wanted different things. Rather than turn and face that, I pushed it under the carpet and figured I could pretend like it wasn't there. Because I was terrified of losing my love, I stuffed my desire for marriage and kids as deep as I could. He had made it clear that they weren't on the menu for him. That's tough, though, because if you're inclined that way, then the more you grow to love someone, the more you want it all. I stopped giving voice to those needs, though. I was worried my ex would call it off and let me go. And while I wanted those thing very badly—I just wanted him more.

If I had known how to read the cards, I believe things would have been different. When I had a major operation for my broken neck, my ex didn't leave my side. He slept on the hospital couch. He looked like the Incredible Hulk, curled up into the fetal position. He wouldn't let anyone send him home. He helped me go to the bathroom, even though it made me want to die with embarrassment. I couldn't stand to feel so needy, even though it seemed to make him so happy to take care of me. I wish I had seen that experience for what it was: an opportunity for me to identify, and then talk about, how undeserving and unworthy I felt, how terrified it made me feel to be dependent. How uncomfortable it makes me feel when I'm not working for affection but instead just basking in love.

Not only did I operate from a place of fear of losing something I wanted (my ex), but I also wanted to be perfect for him because I wanted him to have a perfect life. I so desperately did not want to rock the boat that I threw a lot of things I wanted right out of it. I was continually dishonest about what I wanted—with myself, with my ex—because I was operating out of a place of fear. By continually putting him first, and choking my own voice back, I didn't give him the respect of actually hearing about how I was doing. I didn't given him, or our relationship, the benefit of the doubt that maybe it could handle more. Because I assumed he wasn't willing to make sacrifices, I did not persistently ask. Because I was so fixated on what I believed he wanted, I made many decisions on his behalf, even though I was losing myself in the process.

I don't think it was until I did *Dancing with the Stars* that I really woke up. The producers got me an apartment in Los Angeles for the show, where I stayed for about eleven weeks. It wasn't a palace, but I loved it. I loved doing whatever I wanted, and I loved getting back into my body through dance. I loved hanging out with friends and going out to see live music, brewing a pot of coffee, making an English muffin and some watermelon, choking down my vitamins, turning on the *Today* show. I liked how it felt to be that independent girl. I had been sitting in a jail cell without realizing that the door wasn't locked and that I had built it myself. After *Dancing with the Stars*, I felt like I'd found myself. I didn't want to lose her again.

One of the things that *Dancing with the Stars* also unlocked for me was the idea that I can stand on my own. I think it's partly growing up as a twin, and then becoming a star based on that twindom, but being involved with a mega-star also undermined some of my faith in myself. Brie and I hear it all the time: that we've only gotten the opportunities that have been granted to us because of the guys we're with. Without our men, we wouldn't have our platforms, our prominence within the world of wrestling, our brands—we'd never have been able to become Women's Champions. It's unfair, and it's part of our deeper epidemic as a culture to pull other women down or put their achievements in the context of the men who got them there. I know the Bella Army wants to fight that battle of shifting the perception of women in our sport.

When we made it to the main roster, I was not with my ex. When we landed *Total Divas*, the production crew knew nothing of our relationship. We didn't reveal that he was my boyfriend until the first day of filming. I had built my career for twelve years, and it was painful when people conflated my success with his. My ex never had to stick up for me at WWE. He never had to step in to defend my work or push for me to get more opportunities. That was always done by Vince McMahon, WWE's Chairman and CEO. He recognized that I was popular with the audience, was a good wrestler, and represented the company well.

As our wedding approached, I started to panic. This precedent I had set for myself throughout my life started to rear its head: pleasing others, and stifling what I actually wanted if it didn't match what they wanted. This might sound insane, but I am such a pleaser that when I am not in the position of giving someone exactly what they want, I think that the whole construct breaks. On some deep level, I believe that the only reason I am loved is because of this pleasing. The pleasing is my entire worth. I simply haven't known any other way to be. As our wedding approached, I broke. I simply couldn't stand up to the pressure of making everyone else happy above myself. I panicked. I freaked out. To me, pressure feels like the end of the world. I'm like a wild horse or a feral cat—I'm so used to at least a little bit of dysfunction that anything normal feels like flashing signs of "Danger!"

I had to walk away. I had to let it all go. The fallout was terrible, particularly the speculation within the news media and on social media that it was all for ratings. The thing about reality TV is that you don't get to pick and choose what you show—and the pressure from filming inherently creates drama. It brings things to a head by applying a heavy load to the sensitive parts of your life. Having our relationship fall apart on national TV was excruciating. I had to relive it all again, while also having my heart broken from missing my ex.

I hope our story together will have a happy ending—and in retrospect, I probably wouldn't change anything about it, because I believe I'll end up exactly where I'm supposed to be. But I know the path to get there would have been far less tortured if I hadn't needed to learn a lot of important lessons about tapping into what I want and need and learning how to communicate that to the man I loved most in the world. I don't know what I was scared of, I don't know why I held back. But I can probably attribute some of it to my upbringing, and this disease of pleasing, of not knowing how to just hold love without rushing to give it back. I have also learned how to sit with pain, without covering it up or forcing it to be okay.

If you want something, you have to be willing to call someone to the mat to get it. You have to be willing to take a stand. You state your position and then defend it, even if it means walking out of the arena without the thing you most wanted to win. But if you don't try, if you don't put yourself forward, if you don't lay it all out on the line, then it's nobody's fault but your own if you don't get it. We often operate in relationships like we're with mind readers, like we should all be so tapped into the other person that we can automatically know how they feel. I've found that I sometimes don't even know how *I* feel until I start to give it real voice, to hear how it sounds coming out of my mouth. I think it's like any muscle. As I exercise my voice more and more, it will come easily and often. Love, like everything else, is a nothing ventured, nothing gained situation. Say who you are—say it often and with passion.

# CHAPTER 10

# THE FINISHER

## 2017-2018

Los Angeles, California

San Diego, California

## Nicole

When I was cocktail waitressing in my twenties, one of my legs went dead while I was working a shift. I'd had a lot of pain in my abdomen, which was becoming increasingly unbearable even though I had a really high tolerance for discomfort. I didn't want to go to the hospital or urgent care; I didn't think I could afford it. I decided to wait and see if whatever was happening down there would clear up on its own.

I went home that night and sat in a bath where my flaps were like two floating balls in the water: I was so swollen I looked deformed. It got to the point where I couldn't pee, and I knew I needed medical help, desperately. I went to the hospital, where even the ER nurses were shocked—they all came into the room to take a look at my vagina, like it was a very rare piece of art.

The doctor was a jerk, maybe because I was some twenty-year-old cocktail waitress, maybe because I had bad insurance. He gave me a quick examination and then said: "You have a Bartholin's cyst. You need surgery, but if you expect me to wake up a doctor in the middle of the night for you, you're wrong." And then he left and told me he'd be back to get me set up with morphine. Thirty minutes passed, then forty-five minutes, at which point the pain was so bad I had to yell until someone heard me. A nurse popped her head in and was surprised that I was still there, as the doctor had left without giving them any orders.

The nurses checked me into the hospital and set me up with a morphine drip so that I could manage my pain until I had surgery early the next morning. My phone had died, so I couldn't even call my mom to tell her I was in the hospital. The hospital called her when I was in recovery, which was the first time she heard about this whole debacle. After the operation, which revealed my glands had two cysts, they put two catheters in to drain for two weeks and told me that I'd always be super-sensitive.

I now know how common cysts are for women, but I had no idea to ask about them, and I'd never been checked. I don't know if I would have problems today if I had gotten treatment earlier or had known I could go to a place for a free annual checkup. I still struggle with this issue, and bladder infections are a constant in my life. I also get easily irritated in that area, which is a problem considering that I spend a lot of my days in sweaty workout gear. When we were kids, my mom taught us the birds and the bees, but I didn't learn much about sexual health or how the vagina works. And then I certainly never expected to experience so much sexual trauma, and I was not equipped to deal with that, either.

I also used to slather Victoria Secret scented lotions everywhere—I thought nothing about putting it around, and even on or in, my vagina. Brie and I grew up when girls were terrified that they smelled "down there," when douching and scented tampons seemed like good choices. We were also always waxing and shaving our vaginas, eliminating the protective barrier that can keep harmful bacteria away. It is no surprise that I'm still paying the price.

## Brie

Never one to be one-upped by my sister, I also went to the emergency room for my vagina. When we were living in Los Angeles, after our Hooters days, I went out dancing with some friends and was wearing lace underwear—I don't think they even had a lining. I was about five drinks in, wearing tight-ass jeans, and had a front wedgie. I went to pick it, and a piece of lace was wrapped around my labia, and I tore it.

I went home and slept on it, and the next morning, it was still bleeding so I drove to the emergency room. At check-in, I told the woman I had been injured. She raised an eyebrow: "Yes?

Where?" I pointed down. I was twenty years old, and didn't know any medical terminology, so I told her that I had ripped my vaginal lip—that I didn't know what it was called, but I had ripped my vagina. She looked bemused. She brought me back and asked if I minded that the ER doctor on call was a man. I didn't, but thought it was nice that they had asked.

I told the doctor the story, and he said, "All right, I know that story isn't true." And I said: "Yes, it's true." And he said, "No, you had to have been using a sex toy." And I said, "I wish, but I actually tore my vagina because I picked a front wedgie." Everyone at the hospital thought it was hilarious, and if I'm being honest, I thought it was pretty funny, too. The guy I was dating wasn't amused, because like the doctor, he assumed I had gotten it from using a sex toy—with someone else. By the way, who knew that sex toys can be so dangerous?

The doctor told me that he didn't have to do anything, that the damaged part would fall off—like a lizard's *tail*—and it would regenerate, good as new. I thought he was bullshitting me, but he actually told me the truth. When I got back to my apartment, I had to show all of my girlfriends, because none of them believed me either.

I think one thing that our friends have always appreciated about me and Nicole is that we are very open with our sexuality and our bodies. We aren't shy of, or ashamed by, our body parts. My mom was very open with us from a young age. It would make her crazy that we were so sexual, but she was still adamant about not hiding anything. Because she grew up in a strict, Catholic household, she always hid everything from her parents. And, well, we all know how that turned out. Because she hadn't been educated about protection, she made sure that we were. She wanted to get us on the pill and teach us how to protect ourselves against STDs as soon as she knew that we were sexually active. We were comfortable saying "vagina," "penis," and "sex" because she didn't create a culture of shame around it.

## Nicole

Despite the perpetual physical discomfort, I am a very sexual person. Feeling free to enjoy my sexuality has become a big part of who I am. I want to be part of the movement that shifts all the limiting, old-fashioned beliefs about women—that you can't be a lady and also be sexual, that you can't be taken seriously in business and also care about how you look. For some reason there is this lingering expectation around women that we all only get to be one thing: You can be beautiful, but then not intelligent; you can be sexy, but then you better not be a mom. Men are never criticized or minimized in the same way. It's time that we come together as women and demand that society stop defining us as one thing only.

I like to be sexual, and I like to be sexually dominating, because it makes me feel strong and powerful. I have always been like this. Looking back at my grade school journals, I can see that it was clear then, too. Despite what has happened to me, I have been insistent on embracing it, rather than feeling ashamed. If anything, I have been more determined to find the power in my sexuality because the formative sexual experiences that I had when I was younger left me feeling like I had no power at all.

Many people rush to judge me, to assume that I have allowed and invited men to turn me into an object. On the contrary: I have a lot of respect for myself, and this is who I am. I love having a womanly body, I love having big breasts (even if I wasn't born with them), I love dressing up for myself and feeling sexy. It annoys me to no end when society decides to judge women like me by assuming that high heels and tight dresses mean we don't have any self-respect, or only find value in what men think of us. That is bullshit, and I don't have to wear a potato sack to prove it. I love myself, I respect myself, I am sexual, and I am strong—I can kick anyone's ass. But I would rather do it in Christian Louboutin heels and a bondage dress.

I want younger women to have a different reality, to learn how to take care of themselves so that they don't end up in similar straits. I wish someone had taught me about proper self-care, about keeping things that don't belong in your vagina out of it (scented tampons, fragranced lotions, douches altogether), about wearing organic cotton underwear when you exercise so that your vagina can breathe, about the importance of getting annual physicals to be sure that you don't have untreated cysts or abnormal pap smears. If you don't have insurance, go somewhere where they provide essential services like checkups, breast exams, and pap smears for free. If you have plenty of money, consider making a donation, so another woman can have control over her own health, too.

Being a woman, and owning our femininity, is an incredible source of power. Being a woman means you have the ability to enthrall, the ability to hold, the ability to create. And so much more. Women are awesome, and it's time that we all take our power back—particularly from anyone who wants to take our sexual power away from us or make us feel ashamed for embodying it.

Brie and I knew that we wanted to build a company. We wanted to address female sexuality and empowerment, to create products that were better for vaginas everywhere. Nothing that was going to tear the lip of your vagina, for example, and no products with parabens and phthalates. And in doing that, we also wanted to destigmatize the vagina, to stop girls from giggling about it and inspire them to get to know it!

The name for our lingerie and clothing line, Birdiebee, actually came from the saying "the birds and the bees." We thought the name was cute, but we also wanted to acknowledge how we learn (or don't learn) about sexuality, which has never been taught properly in schools. For example, did you know that the clitoris wasn't even in the 1948 edition of *Gray's Anatomy*, the basic textbook in medical school? In school, we giggled through sex education class, which was about basic anatomy and pregnancy—but nothing about the importance of consent, and nothing about the power of sex to create intimacy and pleasure. And how important it is to own that for yourself, to feel like you can access it. Instead we were left to our own devices, in empty bedrooms at party houses, and there were a lot of missteps. And because of that, a lot of shame. We hope that we can help address that for younger generations.

We believe that there has to be a world where women can be powerful, sexual creatures who can still win respect—where wanting pleasure and equal access to orgasms is not something to feel ashamed about.

## Brie

I had twenty-one hours of labor with Birdie, which ended in an emergency C-section. I pushed for three brutal hours, but my cervix just wouldn't open enough for her fourteen-inch head to make it through.

I was ten days late, and while my doctor knew that I wanted to have her as "naturally" as possible, she had to induce me with Pitocin, which is a drug that starts your contractions. It puts the motion in the ocean. I insisted that I wanted to do the induction without an epidural, which in retrospect seems pretty crazy. Pitocin makes your contractions much more intense, and once the labor gets under way, an epidural is pretty much essential. But as much as my doctor cautioned against going without, she knew it was important to me, so she let me try. I labored for ten hours on Pitocin without an epidural. I have never experienced pain like that. It felt like I was being cut open from the inside. It was exhausting, on every level.

That is not how I had planned it. Like many women who have never had children, I thought I would be able to control the process of bringing Birdie into the world. I wasn't scared of pain, and because of that, I thought I had it in the bag. After all, I jumped off the top ropes in the ring—*clearly* I could handle vaginal birth without drugs. Initially I wanted the full hippie fantasy home birth. I had been taking hypno-birthing classes, I had my doula lined up, and Bryan and I had done tons of research and read every book about having the labor and birth you want.

The thing about kids, though, is that they turn everything upside down. The entire process is an exercise in relinquishing control and understanding that there are forces far greater than you that will dictate how it's going to go. It is an exercise in being willing to just let what will be, be, without any added pressure or expectations. It would have been far more beneficial, it turns out, to take the pressure off Birdie's arrival. All that energy was needed for what would happen after she emerged into the world, like breastfeeding and nourishing my body for the first few months. I wish I had spent that time stocking the freezer with healthy soups, or reading about babies and sleep schedules, and not fixating on the perfect labor that was never going to be in my power to control.

In my mind, my water would break, maybe somewhere like the grocery store—just to make it a good story—and then I would labor at home for a while, holding Bryan's hands and bouncing on my birthing ball. My doula would signal us when it was time to go to the hospital, and then I would push—all in all, a quiet, beautiful, and peaceful birth set to a relaxing soundtrack. My first instinct had been to have Birdie in the bathtub at home, but I was willing to make the concession of going to a hospital so we could be assured of our safety. I thought that by giving up the bathtub, I had made the only concession I needed to make. By not even considering a worst-case scenario, I just set myself up to fail.

Yes, births are important, and they are magical. But the real magic seems to be happening now that Birdie is here, touching every moment of my life. I kind of had it all backwards. I think because I subscribe to living a more natural life, I felt like I had something to prove by having a baby with as little medical intervention as possible. And I don't know what it was exactly that I was trying to prove. In retrospect, the choice of how to approach labor and delivery— a deeply personal decision about what matters to us—has become in my opinion just another part of being a woman where we judge ourselves and each other. We often feel triggered by people who have taken a different path. I don't know how to diffuse that, or just lower the pressure all around. But it feels like women everywhere set themselves up, and are perhaps set up by others, to fail.

The whole situation is loaded with expectation and pressure, when really the abiding rule of law should be to get through it safely. By all means, shoot for the stars and declare the birth story of your dreams, but think of it instead like a birth wish instead of a birth plan. There is no shame if it doesn't work out, and no shame in needing help. I'm kind of inclined to believe, actually, that the more we resist the help, the more the universe will be sure to show us that we need it. The more rigid we are in our expectations, the more the universe will show us that flexibility is a better path. I think about my brother, JJ, and his wife, Lauren. Lauren knew she wanted to give birth to their daughter Vivienne in a hospital. She knew she wanted an epidural, and five hours later, their baby girl was born. She didn't stress herself out; she just picked the path that offered the greatest reward for her—pain-free, fast, and safe. There is a lot of beauty in that.

I have tried not to beat myself up for refusing an epidural earlier. I didn't need to be a hero while I writhed in pain. I was so depleted and so exhausted by the time the pushing started, I wonder if that wasn't part of the reason that I needed to be cut open. I wasn't even awake for my first breastfeeding session. They put her on my chest, and I had already passed out and was snoring. Bryan, Nicole, and my mom were looking around for help—my mom, the only one with any baby experience, didn't breastfeed us, so she had no tips to offer. They just tried to figure it out. Bryan pushed my nipple down while Nicole held Birdie to my boob. That's how motherhood started for me. I wish I had been awake to experience it, if only to see those two bozos trying to milk me.

Because of my C-section, I stayed in the hospital for five days. Hilariously, when I had been preparing for my magical vaginal birth, I was operating under the delusion that I'd be able to set some sort of record and leave the hospital five hours later. The reality was that when it was time to head home, I didn't want to leave. Not only did the nurses teach me everything about taking care of Birdie—different positions for nursing, how to change a diaper, how to swaddle, how to give her a bath—they took incredible care of *me*. I hadn't been aware of how much mothering I would need myself, how good it would feel to have someone focus on how I was doing. I had hired a postpartum doula, who was great, but I really didn't want to leave those nurses.

Besides the transformation of becoming a mother—which really does change your whole world, in both obvious and almost imperceptible ways—the birth experience was really powerful for me precisely because it left me powerless. It taught me that despite my tenacity and resilience throughout life, despite the fact that I want to be able to do anything and everything, there are experiences that I cannot control. Control is a tough issue. Part of becoming a woman, and certainly a mother, I think, is about understanding the give and the take. When Nicole and I were kids, we had no control over anything—our home life, our school life, our future. That lack of control meant that we didn't always feel safe, and certainly we *weren't* always safe. Now that I'm an adult, control feels essential. Because I know that if I'm in the driver's seat, I have the best shot at ensuring that my life will go how I want it to. But in that hospital, I learned that it's okay to give in. It's important to let other people lead when needed, and it's essential to let people take care of you, too.

Finding that balance is really difficult as a woman. I think many of us hold on so tightly because we've never experienced what it can feel like to be really held—to let go for the trust fall and relax into the arms of others, knowing that you're going to be okay. Being a mom has now forced that issue because I know I can't take care of Birdie alone—and I certainly can't take care of Birdie *and* myself alone. I need help and support, like all women everywhere.

I struggled, and Bryan struggled, too. In retrospect, I think he had postpartum depression. It is actually not uncommon among men—even though it is rarely discussed. I had been on a nine-month physical journey of connecting with Birdie: My body was transforming to accommodate her, in real time. He had nothing physical to attach to—he just had books, and he read a lot of them. But no book can prepare you for the real thing—for this tiny, needy creature who has wants and needs that you have to learn on the fly. I got to do the nursing, so his duties were diapering and swaddling. Birdie hated both of those activities with a certain ferocity. It started to wear on him: I had the happy Bird; he had the angry Bird who would have throttled him if she'd had more strength. I also think that he assumed he could just learn, through books and through doing, how to be a dad. But it's not always a natural acclimation or something that you just know how to do. That's another big falsehood in our culture, that it's so "natural" that you take to it without effort. I had to teach him how to be a dad—primarily through admonition and nagging. We didn't have anyone around who could model it for him. It is a tough learning curve, not something to be dismissed.

There seems to be momentum and awareness in the culture building around this idea that parenting is a community endeavor. The cycle of mothering needs to extend far beyond the parent/child relationship—mothers need mothers, too. And fathers need role models. There seems to be a shift as well in the idea that it's much healthier to live our lives without judgment, however well intended that judgment might be.

## Nicole

Speaking of judgment, I've had many well-documented struggles about my own body. For most of our WWE careers, I've been referred to as the "Fat Twin" or the "Chunky Bella." It's a funny thing, because I do like my body. I'm continually amazed by what I'm able to do with it—I've always been an athlete, and I've always been able to rely on it, even when I was wrestling with a broken neck. But it's still a struggle when I'm continually taunted for being ten pounds overweight. The entertainment industry is like that; you can never be thin enough.

I also have to see myself in photographs constantly, and on TV. That old saying that the camera adds ten pounds is true, and it's rough. When you're our height, ten pounds is a lot. When I'm skinnier, I'm more photogenic. If I didn't have to see so many photos, and particularly photos at crazy angles, I wouldn't be so hard on myself. Plus, getting down to my goal weight is tough. It only happens when I'm extremely strict with myself and work out all the time. That's not typically how I like to roll. I love good wine and long dinners out, and I certainly eat too much black licorice. According to people who know me well, I have a raging case of SOMs, which translates to "Start on Monday." I'd just much rather have a great time in the moment.

In the mid-1990s, Sunny was one of the female wrestling stars. She was a manager and she didn't actually wrestle, but she was big-time in WWE because she was the first woman who was part of the company as a pinup—she was a sex symbol for a lot of high school boys. When Brie and I made it to the main stage, she wrote a Facebook post about how she thought I was fat. She wrote: "There's no excuse for any of those girls in their early 20s to get a little chubby. Wait until they hit 35 and everything slows the f–k down. Then what? They are getting paid to look a certain way." She felt terrible about it after, and when she was inducted into the hall of fame, she pulled me aside to apologize. She was clearly nervous to see me. But I don't blame her, either, as it was emblematic of the culture. Wrestling, in particular, is very body oriented. They were always hard on the women who gained five pounds. They would call you into the office and talk to you about it. It has changed now.

## Brie

On the flip side, I have always been a twig—Nicole and Nattie and the other wrestlers would call me a baby deer, because I was so slight compared to some of the other women. I've always been like that, and have always been deliberate about staying that way, which was never that hard until I had Birdie.

I gained close to fifty pounds when I was pregnant, despite the fact that I hiked and moved and ate pretty well throughout. It was a struggle to get it off, even with the support of my trainer, who worked hard to get me back into fighting shape for the ring. The last ten pounds were almost impossible. And because of the C-section, my stomach, which has always been flat and toned, is a mess. I don't know if it will ever be ready to be displayed in public again. But as much as I wanted to hide, I also knew that I needed to reveal my post-baby body in Birdiebee, to show women that like many of them, I was struggling to put myself back together. Too often, women in the spotlight miraculously get the weight off. Or maybe didn't gain much to begin with, but they set a standard that is far from reality for most of us. I wanted women to see that it was hard for me, too. It's been important for me to post shots of my soft mom body in Birdiebee intimates—I've instructed the team not to Photoshop me, either. Instead, I want to show everything. Hopefully, other women can feel connected and know that they're not alone.

I've enjoyed these different seasons of my body, from being tiny and toned to having the world's largest belly for my eight-pound, ten-ounce baby girl, to being a soft 140 pounds now. Before Birdie, I had never weighed more than 130 pounds. This new body is an adjustment, and I'm not comfortable believing that it's permanent. While I've enjoyed this ride, I am looking forward to feeling like myself again, specifically when it's time to go full-on with my wrestling gear, when all parts of you are hanging out in the ring.

I made my first post-Birdie comeback at the *Royal Rumble*. There was no way I could lose my baby weight in time without crash dieting and potentially sacrificing my ability to make breast milk, so I agreed to do it knowing that I would look really different to the fans. I didn't want that to make me say no. It was such a historic night, and it was such an honor to get the phone call—I couldn't say no just because of my vanity. I have worked way too hard for that. Plus, I couldn't imagine explaining to Birdie that I had skipped out on the first ever women's *Royal Rumble* because I felt fat. I will remember that night for the rest of my life, and I hope that other women don't let carrying around a few extra pounds hold them back from doing what they want, either.

I actually enjoyed taking my time with my weight loss. I think it was because when I finally snapped back to normal, it meant that I didn't have a tiny baby anymore, and I'm sad that Birdie is growing up so fast. I also feel like my life has so much meaning now. It's so rich and full. I don't want to spend my days starved and at the gym, missing the whole thing. Between all our brands and businesses, our plates are full. Sometimes at the end of a crazy day, when I know I should work out, I choose to pour myself a glass of wine instead. There are days when you need to say screw the gym in favor of some Cabernet—embrace them!

## Nicole

Just like it's important to let up on the body shaming of women everywhere and to start to project a more inclusive and realistic body image throughout advertising, we also believe that women should have better options when it comes to the quality of the products that they use every day. We believe that it is messed up that the products we put on and in our bodies are full of toxic chemicals that are known carcinogens and endocrine disruptors, and we believe that it is messed up that the FDA doesn't regulate them. When Brie and I started Birdiebee, we wanted to do both basic and beautiful lingerie and loungewear for women that was made from really high-quality fabrics and materials that were free from nasty chemicals. Our end goal is to make sure that everything in the collection is organic, which we're moving toward while keeping an eye on making it affordable. And we want to present the lingerie in a body-positive way, for all women, with all different bodies.

Every woman deserves to feel sexy in her own skin, to be able to fall in love with herself in the mirror whether a guy (or gal) is going to undress her or not. It felt important to us to create a lingerie brand that's by women, for women, that isn't putting forward a totally unrealistic body image, that isn't more about the fantasies of men than the way women want to feel.

## Brie

It's funny, because in our first meeting pitching the concept, Nicole immediately told them that we want to make products from fabrics that are "good for our vaginas." I was trying not to laugh. I think she said vagina twenty times in that first meeting. I could tell that they wanted to react with a "Wow, you are saying the word *vagina!*"—they had a barely perceptible reaction every time she said it. But that was exactly the point: We think that the word *vagina* shouldn't make people blush. No woman should be embarrassed to say it. We've always felt that way. We all come out of them, let's get used to talking about them!

America does a good job of making sex and pleasure a bad, shameful thing. Particularly for young girls. You don't really hear the same condemnation of young boys who might be exploring their penises, and pleasure, and having wet dreams. But there is a lot of shame put on girls for doing exactly the same thing. Girls are not allowed to be into sexual pleasure. It is always portrayed as something illicit, deeply private, and dirty. Because of that, women aren't taught from a young age that it can be beautiful and empowering, that it's natural and important. Instead, being "sexy" is about subjection, or sluttiness, or a guy's pleasure. We need to change that. The conversation needs to focus instead on women who are enjoying their sexuality in an empowered and healthy way, the way that we were all meant to. It is how we were all made! It takes courage and bravery to speak openly about your sexuality in the way that Nicole does. We need more women to do it.

When Nicole and I were first dreaming up our brand, we decided that we wanted something that truly represented us. Being a hippie, I didn't want to make anything that was unnecessary, which is how we settled on essentials and lingerie—everyone needs underwear. And we wanted to put inspirational sayings and people's voices on shirts in order to feed this collective movement of positivity that's happening all around us. We have a platform, and we wanted to walk the walk. We want to build actual products to represent what we're trying to create in the world.

When we were researching fabrics for the intimates line, we were shocked by how many toxic chemicals are in most materials—these are fabrics that you wear close to your body, against your vagina in many cases. We insisted on doing premium fabrics that were free from toxic dyes and chemicals until we could get the line to a place where we could affordably source fabrics that were 100 percent organic. And that's when we had to part ways with Daymond John. We had met Daymond when the Super Bowl was in Phoenix and had fanned out on him hard because we both love *Shark Tank*. We told him we wanted to start a company and he thought we had the chops, but we ultimately had a different vision. Daymond is an awesome guy, and an incredible businessman, but he felt very strongly that we needed to do licensing deals, and that higher-quality fabrics were out of our reach—that they were just too expensive. I had to keep reminding him that I'm a hippie, and that I didn't want to make something solely to slap my name on it. Plus, remember how we react when someone tells us that something can't be done?

Once we were on our own, Nicole went to meet with intimates designers all over Los Angeles. Meantime, I started to drive from factory to factory, learning all that I could about how material is made. Every factory was twenty minutes away from the next and I was newly pregnant and peeing constantly, which means I spent most of the day learning all of the locations of Starbucks bathrooms. Nicole had an educational day, too, particularly when she asked the lingerie designer if she could turn around the collection the following week. As we've learned, doing things right takes much longer than that!

In the end, I'm grateful to Daymond John because our parting ways made me get off my ass and go experience everything first-hand. We ended up touching the whole process, taking control of our product, and getting to know every nook and cranny of the business, including the ins and outs of the factories. We needed to understand how it all has to come together in order to make the thing you want. Business can be intimidating, particularly for two women who never went to a four-year college and have a far-from-typical career trajectory. But it has been really empowering to force ourselves to learn things, to not be intimidated by all that we don't know. And the reality is, like with most things, it's far less complicated than people want you to believe. It's primarily about following your gut. We had already spent a year developing the line, and in the course of a few days, we realized that we had to start over. We needed to redesign the products to feel more like us, and we needed to source better fabrics. But it's been worth it; it was a blessing in disguise.

We still have a lot to learn. It has been challenging to try to run a company while wrestling for WWE and filming two TV shows. If we had it to do over, I would insist on controlling every part of the process even if it took us longer to launch. There are a lot of things that need to line up exactly right. At the beginning, it's key to make it as close to your vision as possible, so that the people who work for you understand what you want and can then rinse and repeat. And it's also hard and expensive to fix things after the fact. Because we're going for higher-quality materials, we've also struggled to keep the price point as low as we would like for our fans—when we launched, they were pissed. They felt like we had left them out by making everything too expensive. I wish we had better communicated why. We worked really hard to make sure that the materials were right, and we priced it all as low as we could from that. It was hard not to feel bummed out that our fans were so disappointed. I'm sure they felt like it was arbitrary, that we were just trying to make a quick buck, because we didn't explain ourselves well.

We were also both very adamant about including plus sizes at launch and showing a wide range of ethnicities and skin tones. But we couldn't get it lined up for the launch—we didn't have the plus-size samples in time to be photographed, we didn't insist on signing off on the models that had been chosen, and we had already announced the launch date to the press and our fans. When we saw the launch photography and realized everyone was skinny and blond, we should have pushed it back and insisted on a reshoot, but we felt like the train had left the station. It was a misfire. Knowing what I know now, I realize that it would have been a better message to be honest about the delay than to put up with Birdiebee leaving out a lot of our fans, but we felt pushed into launching anyway. As we move forward, we are trying to do much better. As we learn more and more, we are feeling increasingly confident in our ability to trust our guts and make the right calls for the business.

Our long-term goal is to move into feminine hygiene products, to create organic tampons and wipes and lubes that are sex- and body-positive, and completely free from toxins. That are 100 percent safe or even actively good for you. As soon as we have the intimates and loungewear in hand, we will move on to that.

Part of the learning curve has been understanding how to hire, and when to fire. Building a team is really hard. We've found that just because we like someone, or they do nice stuff for us, doesn't mean that they're the perfect fit. We have needed to harden our hearts a little bit. We can't be so taken with gestures that we don't see through to what best serves the business. It's tough because we both have huge hearts. I think it goes back to our childhood, those cherished moments when someone was nice to us, or showed us some kindness. It's hard not to let that affect the business when difficult decisions need to be made.

## Nicole

It shouldn't come as a surprise, but making wine is a whole lot more pleasurable than making T-shirts—though it takes a long-ass time to do it right, too. If you've watched even one episode of *Total Divas* or *Total Bellas*, then you know that Brie and I are winos. We have always enjoyed a glass of red at the end of a long day, even when it was $4.99 from the bar at the Holiday Inn Express. You could say that Belle Radici and Bonita Bonita, our wine companies, have been in the making since we were sneaking drinks underage, though during our Hooters days, we were still drinking Bud Light.

We grew up in a farming and agriculture family. We spent much of our childhood down in Brawley, California, where our Pop Pop's fledgling produce cart from Philadelphia had become an intergenerational company. The earth has always been in our blood. As we took more and more trips to Napa to drink wine and relax, we became increasingly interested in how wine is made, and the agricultural practices behind it. When we met Ryan Hill, of Hill Family Estate, a vineyard that makes some of the best wines in the region (and supplies grapes to many of the other incredible makers in the area), it felt like fate. Like us, Ryan grew up in a family of people who worked the earth, though their singular focus was on grapes, whereas our family touches everything from oranges to asparagus.

We wanted to make really beautiful wines and then bring them to the Bella Army at a really good price—since we could sell the wine straight from the site, we could cut out the middle man. And incredibly, we blew out both of our wines within thirty-six hours—the red blend was all gone in fifteen hours. The launch went way beyond our expectations, and we were elated to read comments that people were as into the wine as we were. Since then we've introduced a Chardonnay and a rosé, which also sold out immediately.

Belle Radici and Bonita Bonita seem quite distinct from Birdiebee, but the way we think about the empire that we want to build, they're not. Both our wine companies and our lifestyle brand are predicated on the idea of celebrating life, of looking for any occasion, whether it's a date night or a family gathering, to wear something that makes you feel good, eat something delicious, and top it off with an incredible bottle of wine. We want to relish life's small pleasures, in all the details that make us feel like empowered women.

The TV shows, the Instagram followers, the general interest in what we do is so worth it if it means that we get to change the world. It isn't surprising that a lot of people assume Brie and I are in the wrestling game because we want to be famous; but we're actually in this because we want to be successful. When we were young and living with our parents in Arizona, all Brie and I wanted was to stand on our own two feet, to have control over our futures and our destinies. We wanted to be in charge of our own happiness. If fame were all we were after, there are easier ways to get there than throwing yourself around in a ring in a canned food factory. We were getting enough small breaks then that we probably would have been able to string something together as twin actresses. But that's not what we wanted—we wanted to change the world.

We have always longed for real connection—not sympathy. So before this book we held back a lot of our story. We never wanted anyone to assume that we got where we've gotten because we leveraged what happened to us in our past. We never wanted to build our following on victimhood or play that card, so to speak. But we'd also be lying if we said that everything that has happened to us hasn't landed us right where we are. It certainly made us stronger and tougher, and it made us want success more. We both had nothing to lose, and everything to gain.

I think that people who know us now will be surprised by these pages. They may be surprised that there's so much pain in our history and that we're so positive despite it all. I think we've worked hard, and will continue to work hard throughout our lives, to process everything in a way that is healthy, to spin pain into gold. While trauma has been part of our story, we don't want it to become the defining plotline, ever. I hope that readers who have suffered similar things in their own pasts will read these pages and know that they're not alone. We don't have to stay in the darkness. Hopefully we can learn from our mistakes, from our experiences. Brie and I both feel like we're here to be teachers and guides. We live our lives like an open book so that others can learn from, or see themselves in, our life stories. And see how we have not only survived but thrived.

Now that wrestling full-time is no longer an option for me, I'm anxious to try new things. I'd love to have a talk show with Brie someday where we can drink wine and have fun conversations with strangers, or even have a wine show. Or maybe even do some acting. We also want to run our own production company so that we can be the deciding voice in the room and have full creative control. We want to be able to put shows and movies out there that get overlooked, or have great meaning. I would love to be more of an activist for what I believe in.

## *Brie*

As has been said by many wise people in the world (and many bumper stickers): Be the change you want to see in the world. We feel like we've been put on earth to do exactly that. If we can change just one person's life, then it's worth it. We are pleasers, and we take care of other people first. That has fueled us to work around the clock. We want to make enough to share, to be able to buy our friends dinner when they're stretched, to give someone a spare bedroom to crash in when they have nowhere else to go, to help the animals and the earth. We live happy, comfortable lives because we're always giving. We try not to keep it all for ourselves. I'm grateful for every day that I get to breathe. You only get so much time, so let's make every moment count.